ARLEN R

HEAVY METAL GUITAR

ns
ARLEN ROTH'S
HEAVY METAL GUITAR

ARLEN ROTH

SCHIRMER BOOKS
A Division of Macmillan, Inc.
NEW YORK

Collier Macmillan Canada
TORONTO

Maxwell Macmillan International
NEW YORK   OXFORD   SINGAPORE   SYDNEY

Copyright © 1991 by Schirmer Books
    A Division of Macmillan, Inc.

All rights reserved. No part of this book may be reproduced or
transmitted in any form or by any means, electronic or mechanical,
including photocopying, recording, or by any information storage
and retrieval system, without permission in writing from the
Publisher.

Schirmer Books
A Division of Macmillan, Inc.
866 Third Avenue, New York, N.Y. 10022

Collier Macmillan Canada, Inc.
1200 Eglinton Avenue East, Suite 200
Don Mills, Ontario M3C 3N1

Library of Congress Catalog Card Number: 89-14519

Printed in the United States of America

printing number
  2 3 4 5 6 7 8 9 10

Library of Congress Cataloging-in-Publication Data

Roth, Arlen.
    [Heavy metal guitar]
    Arlen Roth's heavy metal guitar / by Arlen Roth.
        p.   cm.
    Discography: p.
    ISBN 0-02-870010-4
    1. Electric guitar—Methods (Heavy metal) 2. Heavy metal (Music)—
Instruction and study. I. Title.
MT582.R814 1991
787.87'193166—dc20   89-14519
                                                                    CIP
                                                                    MN

For Deborah, Gillian, and Alexis

Contents

Acknowledgments	xi
Introduction	xiii

ONE
EQUIPMENT — 1

Guitars for Heavy Metal Playing	1
The Parts of an Electric Guitar	2
Three Great Classics: The Telecaster, the Stratocaster, and the Les Paul	3
Modern Heavy Metal Guitars	6
Pickups	12
Strings	12
Picks	13
Amplifiers	14
Effects Boxes	18

TWO
READING TABLATURE, SYMBOLS, AND STANDARD NOTATION — 21

Rhythmic Notation	22
Tablature	26
Symbols	26

THREE
FUNDAMENTALS OF HEAVY METAL TECHNIQUE   31

The Right Hand	31
The Left Hand	32
Exercises for Developing Right and Left Hand Coordination	33
Stretches for the Fourth Finger	36
Basic Blues/Rock Scales	37
Sliding Between Notes	38

FOUR
THE INFLUENCE OF EARLY ROCK AND BLUES   41

Shuffle Patterns	41
String Bending	47
Blues Licks	51
Major Pentatonic Licks	54
Hammer-ons and Pull-offs	57
Vibrato	59
Starting to Put it all Together	61
SOME BLUES GREATS	66
ROBERT JOHNSON	66
OTIS RUSH	68
BUDDY GUY	70
B.B. KING	72
MIKE BLOOMFIELD	74

FIVE
EARLY HEAVY METAL RHYTHM GUITAR   77

Power Chords	77
Power Chord Progressions	77

More Advanced Power Chord Positions	81
Pete Townshend's Right Hand Flourishes	82
The Constant Bass Technique	84

SIX
EARLY HEAVY METAL LEAD GUITAR — 87

"Overbending"	87
Early Heavy Metal "Flash"	90
Your First Heavy Metal Lead Solos	92
ROCK'S FIRST "GUITAR GODS"	97
JIMMY PAGE	97
JIMI HENDRIX	99
ERIC CLAPTON	101

SEVEN
CONTEMPORARY HEAVY METAL GUITAR — 103

The Various Scale Modes	104
Improvising Using the Modes	112
The Harmonic Minor Scale	118
The Vibrato or "Whammy" Bar	123
Whammy Bar Exercises	124
Using Harmonics in Heavy Metal Guitar	129
Right-Hand Tapping	133
STEVE VAI: A CONTEMPORARY METAL MASTER	147

EIGHT
DOUBLE AND HARMONY GUITAR SOLOING — 157

NINE
ARPEGGIATING YOUR SOLOS — 163

MODAL ARPEGGIOS — 168
   TWO-HANDED TAPPING ARPEGGIOS — 168
   RANDY RHOADS — 170

TEN
FORMING AND WORKING WITH A BAND — 175

Rehearsing — 176
Performing — 177

ELEVEN
YOUR CONTINUED GROWTH — 181

Discography — 183

Acknowledgments

There were many people who helped make this book possible, and they truly deserve special thanks. First I must thank Joe Dalton for helping with the music, and John Frusciante for transcribing Steve Vai's solos. I also want to thank Vinnie Moore, Vivian Campbell, Steve Vai, Fred Weiler, Ebet Roberts, Tom Hroncich, my wife Deborah, Ned Steinberger, Kaman Music, Jay Jay French, Scholz Research and Development, and one of the best and most patient editors under the sun, Maribeth Anderson Payne.

Introduction

Over the last few years, heavy metal music has enjoyed a resurgence in popularity unsurpassed by previous comebacks of this style. For the first time it has truly interwoven itself into the mainstream of popular music. The instrument that has always been at the heart of the heavy metal sound is the guitar. This book will address the guitar's intriguing development into the staple that it is today.

Heavy metal first developed in the late 1960s largely as a loud form of blues playing. Blues enjoyed an enormous growth in popularity during the mid to late 1960s, particularly among white audiences. "Heavy" groups such as Mountain, Led Zeppelin, Cream, and The Jeff Beck Group developed directly out of the amplified Chicago Blues medium. Blues songs were either redone in a heavier, slower fashion, or new songs were composed, creating an even more eclectic "heavy metal" approach. Several guitarists were to emerge at this time who were to change forever the way we think of electric guitar playing, particularly in the heavy metal, or loud blues, format. These guitarists were Leslie West, Jeff Beck, Jimi Hendrix, Eric Clapton, and Jimmy Page. Jimi Hendrix and Jeff Beck were perhaps the most experimental, though they were both great straight blues players as well. Eric Clapton and Jimmy Page were more traditional, and their playing has always shown a direct influence from Chicago players such as Otis Rush, Buddy Guy, and B.B. King. Jimmy Page's band, Led Zeppelin, probably did more to popularize and define the heavy metal sound in the late 1960s and early 1970s than any other single band. Led Zeppelin's strong influence is still felt today in the music of nearly anyone who plays in this genre.

The mid-1970s saw a continuation of the heavy metal medium, particularly in England, with bands such as Judas Priest and Black Sabbath leading the way. Though they enjoyed some success, for the most part these bands featured rather uninventive guitar playing that was simply a continuum of the "loud blues" approach. This was the period that led to the so-called "devil-worship" theatrical approach to heavy metal—black leather, metal studs, and the like. Unfortunately, this was what a lot of "metal" music was comprised of: lots of show, but little musicianship.

Throughout the 1980s, however, this all changed, and the heavy metal genre has grown to include some of rock music's most gifted musicians, especially guitarists. These players have become the foremost guitar heroes of the day. Players such as Eddie Van Halen, Yngwie Malmsteen, Steve Vai, Ritchie Blackmore, and a host of others have shot a burst of life into contemporary guitar playing with their inventiveness, creativity, and showmanship. As a

Introduction

result, kids today are much more apt to make their first guitar purchase a fire-engine-red Strat with a whammy bar rather than the gut-stringed "folk" guitar of the more simplistic days. They're also inclined to be tackling more difficult pieces of music than their forerunners, as metal is becoming very demanding, and there are many difficult tricks to maneuver. Right-hand "tapping," harmonics, feedback, and other advanced techniques are de rigueur in heavy metal playing, so we'll cover all of this material in the pages that follow.

As a student of the roots of rock guitar, and having raised myself with a need to go to the source in all guitar playing, I believe it is important to discuss the various techniques and styles that led up to today's complex heavy metal approach. It is a bad mistake (and many make it) to take Yngwie Malmsteen's guitar playing as "square one" in one's understanding of the historical development of rock guitar. He wouldn't be standing there wailing away on his Strat had Hendrix not done so before him, nor Duane Eddy before him, nor Robert Johnson before him . . . you get the picture. Blues is at the heart of all rock music, and though many books have been written on the subject (mine included), I think it's important that in this book we cover some of this crucial and fundamental art form. This will help you gain a greater insight into heavy metal guitar and where it all came from. I feel it's important that your own development go through some of the same evolution that the guitar itself has undergone over the last thirty years or so. We will study the early heavy metal styles of the 1960s and early 1970s, and also will take an in-depth look at some of contemporary heavy metal's most challenging techniques and styles.

As the techniques grow and expand, it seems that the supply of equipment that is available to the musician does also. There is a more complex array of guitars, amplifiers, and effects these days than anyone would've dreamed possible fifteen years ago. I would like to help you sort through all the mess and arrive at what is truly necessary for you to sound the way *you* want to. To this end, I've devoted a chapter in this book to choosing the right guitar, amp, and other equipment for your needs.

Over the last twenty-six years or so, I've gone through just about every experience one can go through as a guitarist. I've amassed a lot of knowledge and have learned a lot the hard way. I hope that by passing this knowledge on to you, I may head off some of the "growing pains" and trial-and-error experiences that could slow you down. I hope that you grow and blossom at a very early age, because the guitar is an eternally youthful instrument that, in youthful hands, can become a force that the rest of the world must reckon with. Good luck, and on with the playing!

ARLEN ROTH'S

HEAVY METAL GUITAR

Equipment

GUITARS FOR HEAVY METAL PLAYING

Throughout the book, I will help guide you to make the right decision about buying a guitar, and hopefully uncover some of the mysteries behind what makes these instruments "tick." While examining the different types of guitars and guitar equipment, I must use terms which may be unfamiliar to you. I will define or illustrate these terms when they appear in boldface later in the book, so don't be discouraged if you don't understand everything at first.

When one walks into a music store these days, one can't help but be amazed at the barrage of various shapes, colors, and styles of electric guitars that are available. Now more than ever, guitars are fashion too. To many people, it's not only how the instrument plays and sounds, but also how it looks that is carefully considered when making a purchase. This was always true to a certain extent, but there never was the vast *selection* that is available today. For those who don't know better, this can be very confusing as well as frustrating. It seems that the importance placed on a guitar's flashy appearance hinders one's ability to determine whether the guitar sounds and plays right. Attaining this ability is difficult, for it takes time to develop your playing to the point of being able to make these decisions on your own. When shopping for a guitar it certainly helps to have someone with you who has some experience with guitars. I've helped many students make the proper choice for their guitars, and I've seen that making the right choice is very important, especially when it comes to continuing on happily with their studies.

One problem that exists when buying a guitar is, as when you shop for a car, your mind may be already made up—sometimes for the wrong reasons—before you even walk into the showroom. You may be convinced, for example, that you want to buy a Flying V guitar like your hero Michael Schenker plays, before you've played one to determine whether or not it is even *possible* for you to play such an extreme instrument. You may also be swayed by an advertisement that carries a certain guitarist's endorsement of a particular instrument that, although perfect for him, may be the worst guitar imaginable for you.

There are certain leading manufacturers in the heavy metal guitar market that have at least proven themselves worthy contenders for your dollar. These manufacturers are ESP, Kramer, Guild, Charvel/Jackson, Ibanez, Yamaha, Schecter, and of course, Fender and Gibson. There are scores of smaller companies making fine guitars as well, but they are far too numerous and ever-changing to be named here. Suffice to say that there are plenty of guitar makers to choose from that provide enough models to suit any guitarist's needs.

THE PARTS OF AN ELECTRIC GUITAR

Before we continue our discussion on which guitar is right for you, we must first establish a working knowledge of the guitar and its parts. For this purpose, I've provided this picture illustrating all of the parts of the guitar.

There are several types of electric guitars that don't necessarily apply to heavy metal playing, such as jazz-style hollow-bodies and acoustic/electrics, so our discussion will concentrate solely on the solid-body style of guitar.

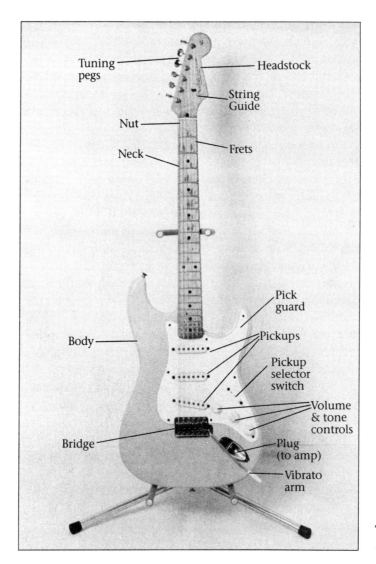

The Parts of a Guitar.

THREE GREAT CLASSICS: THE TELECASTER, THE STRATOCASTER, AND THE LES PAUL

One thing has always amazed me. The first *three* production solid-body electric guitars ever marketed for mass consumption—namely Fender's Telecaster and Stratocaster, and the Gibson Les Paul—are to this day the most popular guitar types, having endured decades of changing musical styles. It's a tribute to the work these early inventors put into their instruments, and it also illustrates the electric guitar's basic simplicity and purity of function-as-design. Before going on to some of the later designs, let's examine these true guitar classics.

The Fender Telecaster

Though many people lay claim to inventing the solid-body electric, Leo Fender's Telecaster (or Broadcaster as it was first called) made history as the first production solid-body in 1948. A guitar of exquisite simplicity, it has long been sought after for its searing, biting tone, and its wonderful sustain. It has frequently been found in the hands of some of the best rock players, but it has been most closely associated with the "twangy" sounds of country music. It is one of the best guitars for sound at low as well as high volumes. I would highly recommend owning this instrument, especially if you can find one of the very desirable (and expensive) early models from 1948 to 1966. If not, there are many manufacturers who are replicating the authentic early style Telecaster including Fender itself, ESP, and Schecter. If you have a later model, the authentic "vintage" sound can also be achieved by replacing the pickups with something like Seymour Duncan brand pickups. Duncan is dedicated to replicating the early sounds as well as creating new ones, and with his pickups a guitar can be made into almost anything possible! Here is a picture of my favorite guitar, a 1953 Fender Telecaster. Note its one-piece maple neck.

1953 Fender Telecaster.

The Fender Stratocaster

In late 1953, the Stratocaster became the second solid-body electric guitar introduced to the public by Fender. A vastly different instrument, it had three pickups rather than the usual two, and in most cases contained a vibrato arm. Since its inception, and especially in the last fifteen years, the "Strat" has arguably become the most popular electric guitar ever produced, aided by its high visibility in the hands of Jimi Hendrix, Eric Clapton, and Mark Knopfler. This guitar, with its wide tonal capabilities, is still a major force in heavy metal, as witnessed by its use by Yngwie Malmsteen, Ritchie Blackmore, and Gary Moore. It first gained widespread popularity when played by many of the "surf-sound" musicians of the early 1960s such as Dick Dale, The Ventures, The Surfaris, and The Beach Boys, before its impact on rock music was understood. It should also be pointed out that Hank Marvin of The Shadows, a legendary British guitarist who influenced countless players in England, was the first to use a Stratocaster there and was largely responsible for its enormous popularity.

Not only is the Strat the most popular guitar in history, but it's also the most imitated and embellished guitar in contemporary guitar building. After many players started "hot-rodding" their Strats in the late 1960s and early 1970s with double-coil humbucking pickups among other things, the manufacturers started to take notice. Soon they were producing what were basically still Stratocasters, but with different pickup configurations, tonal possibilities, new vibrato bar assemblies, and new woods and finishes. Of course, if you went through the trouble, you could literally "build" a new guitar with all of

A trio of vintage Stratocasters: left to right, 1958, 1954, 1957.

the replacement parts on the market today. Or you could simply choose from one of the "hot-rods" being offered by Charvel/Jackson, Yamaha, Schecter, ESP, Guild, or one of the other fine companies that now offer guitars in literally every setup imaginable.

I've always been somewhat of a traditionalist when it comes to instruments, and as in the case of the Telecaster, I wholeheartedly recommend that you make a Strat part of your guitar arsenal. Even if it must be your only guitar, it will offer a wider tonal variety than most other instruments, and will certainly open many creative doors for you. I know it did for me!

The Gibson Les Paul

When it comes to true volume and that "fat" sound so many metal players try to achieve, nothing can really touch the Les Paul. It was the first production solid-body electric introduced by the Gibson company in 1952, and its inventor, the legendary Les Paul, is one of the last of his breed to make a permanent impact on the way guitars and *all* music will be forever played, recorded, and heard.

Though the original Les Paul only had single-coil pickups like its Fender competitors, Gibson soon introduced its renowned double-coil "humbucker" pickups in the mid-1950s. This pickup canceled out "hum" by having two coils of wire instead of one. Because of its wider magnetic field, it produced a chunkier, "fatter" tone that soon became popular with rock and blues players. This is the sound most often associated with the Les Paul, and with Gibsons in general, and early models with "patent-applied-for" humbucker pickups are extremely rare, desirable, and expensive! Many well-known Gibson electrics received the humbuckers as well, such as the Flying V, The Explorer, and the SG, but none of these instruments achieved the notoriety or popularity of the Les Paul.

After 1960, the Les Paul model was canceled and its name (much to the chagrin of its namesake) was affixed to an entirely new model called the SG. Soon after, however, the name was dropped entirely, and not until the Les Paul became a cult guitar again in the late 1960s was it reintroduced as it had existed in the 1950s. As its popularity continued to grow in the 1970s, the Les Paul was offered in several styles. Les Paul himself even resumed an active role in helping Gibson develop more guitars, and instruments such as the Les Paul Recording model were the result.

I would recommend owning a Les Paul or Les Paul-type guitar if you are interested in heavy metal guitar playing. However, there are some possible drawbacks you should know about. In most cases, the Les Paul is an extremely *heavy* instrument that can really take its toll on your back during the course of a performance or recording session. Also, although its sound is fat and punchy, it tends to be a bit more limited in its tonal capabilities than the Fenders, so be aware of this when making your guitar choices. One very good alternative that avoids these problems is getting one of the many instruments that contain various pickup combinations that were previously unavailable unless you did some "hot-rodding" yourself. We'll discuss the various pickups and their sounds later in this chapter.

Equipment

1952 Les Paul Standard.
(bridge unoriginal)

MODERN HEAVY METAL GUITARS

Today's guitarist is faced with a veritable cornucopia of wild instruments to choose from, sometimes making shopping for one a nightmare. Certain qualities and on-board equipment seem to have become the norm for guitars that are used primarily for heavy metal music. For example, extremely wide, flat fingerboards and thin necks have become more common due to the popularity of right-handed tapping as well as the more "over-the-fingerboard" almost "classical" way in which much of heavy metal is played these days.

The vibrato bar has also become a mainstay, and it's hard for a young player these days to imagine a new guitar without one. These units used to cause terrible tuning problems in the old days, but manufacturers such as Floyd Rose and Kahler have pioneered special locking vibrato systems that keep the guitar from getting out of tune, thereby opening the doors to wilder and freer "whammy bar" technique. Though these locking systems do work, they have some disadvantages. For one, they simply add an awful lot of extra weight and hardware to your instrument. Some break strings too often, and they make little tricks behind the nut of the guitar (one of my specialties) impossible. There is help on the way, however. Systems that can eliminate tuning problems without monopolizing the entire instrument are being perfected!

Equipment

Kahler "locking" style tremolo system installed in a Guild guitar.
Photo by Jay Abend courtesy of Guild Guitars.

The famous "headless" Steinberger guitar, revolutionary in itself, has now incorporated an incredible "transposing" tremolo bar that actually lowers or raises all the strings in perfect tune with each other. The bar can also be locked into various positions, keeping the instrument re-tuned to that lower or higher pitch. This is another Steinberger innovation that's bound to affect music greatly.

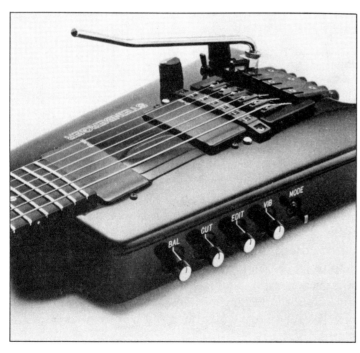

Steinberger guitar with Trans-Trem, or transposing tremolo arm.

Equipment

Though many of the guitar shapes you'll see these days appear quite outlandish, their odd shapes can result in some of the best-balanced instruments to play. Most guitars based upon the Explorer shape (the Explorer was an ill-fated experiment by Gibson in 1958 that has since become a rare collectors item), for example, are beautifully balanced and well suited to both sitting and standing. This is not the case with many instruments, as many seem to slip away from you when playing in a seated position. The Firebird guitar was a more subdued design that was influenced by the more radical Explorer, and was far more successful for Gibson. Many of the vintage ones are still around and, in fact, both the reverse Firebird and the Explorer are being produced again.

A rare transitional 1965 Firebird. Early reverse body, later nonreverse headstock.

The Flying V is another story, however. Its radical shape only caught on a little more than the Explorer's, but playing it in the seated position was nearly impossible. In the early days, artists such as Lonnie Mack and Albert King gave the V a lot of exposure, and now it is one of the most popular guitar styles of all, despite its discomfort, thanks to artists such as Michael Schenker and many other heavy metal influentials. Of course, this was another Gibson guitar to feature the humbucking pickups, and is once again being made in large quantities. It can be a real flash guitar, but beware of its physical drawbacks.

Equipment

Carlos Cavazo of Quiet Riot playing a late model Gibson Flying V.
© Ebet Roberts, 1983.

Charvel/Jackson, ESP, Kramer, and Steinberger are powerful, new names on the guitar scene, and they're making a point of catering to today's guitarists' needs with futuristic designs, materials, and other properties. During the past decade, smaller companies such as these sprang up everywhere to help fill an almost "emergency" need on the part of guitarists for well-crafted, unique instruments. Many of these companies have emerged to become giants of the industry, with endorsements by today's top artists.

As I mentioned earlier, companies like Kramer, Jackson, and Guild have started building guitars with heavy metal almost exclusively in mind. The wide, flat fingerboards reflect the trends in technique. The following is an assortment of some of these modern instruments. Note how some are unique, while many still play on the old themes of the Les Paul, Telecaster, or the Stratocaster.

Brand-new ESP Strat copy; a fine, low-priced guitar.

An interesting contemporary play upon the traditional Telecaster theme by ESP. Note locking tremolo system.

Japanese-made ESP Navigator. A fine Les Paul look-alike.

Wild finishes have really caught on in heavy metal.

It can fly, but does it play?

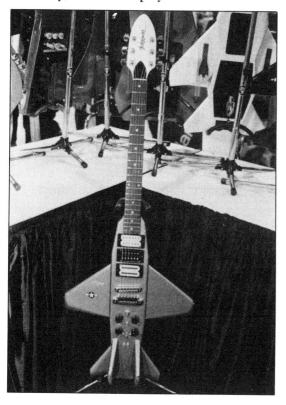

B. C. Rich has long been associated with wild body styles.

Another interesting finish by ESP, popularized by Bruce Kulick of Kiss.

11

PICKUPS

As far as your sound goes, no single component of the electric guitar can have as much of an effect as the pickup. There are many types and manufacturers, but they basically fall into two categories—single- or double-coil. Single-coil pickups, as often found on Fender-type guitars, tend to have a clearer, brighter tone, while double-coil pickups are noticeably warmer and "dirtier." Two coils also cancel out the "hum" interference that can plague single-coil guitars, as in the case of the Gibson humbucker. Seymour Duncan came up with an ingenious double-coil "stacked" pickup that retains the brilliance and clarity of a single-coil pickup, while canceling out the "hum." This makes a great replacement pickup for Teles and Strats, and there is no need to rout out extra wood for their installation.

Many new guitars are being offered with a combination of both single and double-coil pickups, but even better, some manufacturers actually offer pickups that can be switched on and off between single and double-coil modes. This is a very useful feature to have, and I employ it on many of my instruments. It is particularly popular on many of the single-pickup "stark" instruments that are popular in heavy metal, so that you can get two distinct sounds from one pickup. When testing a guitar of this kind, make sure that the single-coil sound is not too thin or "glassy." You want it to retain some of the warmth of the double-coil setting, while at the same time adding the clarity and bite that the single-coil can create. There are many ways that a guitar can be set up to make this kind of switching possible—usually either a switch mounted near the controls, or sometimes a control that activates the single-coil sound when pulled up. I prefer the latter, for it keeps the appearance of the guitar simpler and requires less work to install.

Many of the major pickup manufacturers produce pickups that are suitable for heavy metal, but some offer more than others. For example, EMG has become extremely popular among metal players, but I find it to be a rather flat sounding pickup that only works well at extremely loud volumes or with lots of effects. Seymour Duncan and DiMarzio, however, offer a much broader selection of sounds catering to many different tastes, and their pickups tend to have more depth and character in their sound.

STRINGS

Choosing which gauge string you use for your guitar playing is largely a matter of personal preference, but many times you may be using the wrong set for what you'd like to be getting out of your guitar. I can recall in my late teens, practicing my beloved string bending in a music shop in Manhattan's Greenwich Village. At that time I was using extra-light gauge strings with the high E string a thickness of .009. The fellow who was minding the store noted that I was bending so well and with such ease that I might be well-advised to step up to the next higher gauge (.010), giving me more sustain

Equipment

and power out of the guitar. Not only was he right, but it was a change that was to improve forever the way I sounded and played. In addition, I was able to increase the strength in my fingers for bending and vibrato.

In many cases, however, heavy metal is a different story. I have found that almost all metal players seem to prefer .009's on their axes, due to the use of flatter fingerboards and right-hand tapping. The lighter gauge doesn't resist the tap as much as the heavier gauge does, and usually their amplification is so loud and the pickups so strong that the lightness of the string gauge is hardly noticeable. The problems I find are that the lighter strings become harder to "dig into" with the pick for an aggressive attack and tone, and that they tend to break more often than .010's. Experiment to find which is best for you. I recommend light gauge (.010's) most of all, but I have no objection to extra-lights, as long as they feel right for you. Besides, you can always "step-up" to lights as I did when you feel strong enough. The improvement in sound will be quite noticeable when you do!

PICKS

Guitar picks come in an endless array of sizes, shapes, and thicknesses. Some of them you'll recognize in the photo that follows. The most common type used is the triangle with two rounded edges, but many metal players prefer the larger, more massive picks such as the large triangle shape. This enables you to "dig in" more to the strings, and makes power chord work easier. If

**A star-studded collection of picks.
Note the various shapes available.**

Equipment

you prescribe to the lightning-fast picking school of metal playing, where you don't do many hammer-ons or pull-offs, you may want to use a pick of heavy thickness. This doesn't bend as easily when touching the string, enabling you to fly across the strings with far more ease. In fact, there have been many other materials used for this kind of pick to increase its weight even further, such as stone and copper. Some guitarists even use coins! I wouldn't go that far, as coins don't have the right kind of edge for attacking the string, and could result in a lot of breakage.

AMPLIFIERS

Amplifiers are a major subject when it comes to heavy metal, because it is probably the most *amplified* form of music on the face of the earth! We have all seen the archetypical metal band with stacks and stacks of Marshall amps behind them, playing with literally deafening volume. I've gone to see some groups where the only way I could discern the notes they were playing was by covering my ears!

Seriously, though, the amp is a very important tool for the guitarist, and the one you choose can make a big difference in your sound. In this section I examine some of the various types of amps to help you to come to a decision about which type is right for you.

Small Amplifiers

Although heavy metal is usually thought of as a medium for large amps, smaller amplifiers have always been an integral part of studio work in rock music. Smaller amps are being made these days with features that enable them to be overdriven to obtain that sought-after "dirty" sound for loud rock music. Of course, these work best in close-miked situations where you have either a recording studio, or an extremely sensitive P.A. system. Most live heavy metal situations require a large amplifier set-up.

There are many companies making smaller amps for home and studio use that deliver nearly authentic overdriven heavy metal sound. Yamaha, Peavey, and even Marshall, the king of heavy metal amps, are making small amps that can replicate the heavy metal sound at lower, more tolerable volumes.

One major advance was scored by Tom Scholz of the group Boston, who invented the Rockman headphone amplifier. This is an incredible device, with state-of-the-art sound. You can now plug in, put the headphones on, and sound as if you're in a stadium. It has several very usable "cleaner" settings as well as fine built-in chorus and reverb effects. It can be plugged directly into a board or tape deck for recording, or used as a pre-amp to a larger amplifier, enhancing its sound. Many of the solos of Billy Gibbons (from ZZ Top) simply utilize the Rockman plugged directly into the board!

When choosing the right small amp, it's important that there are certain features present. Reverb is essential, as is a regular volume *and* master volume control. These two volume controls can be regulated to create just the right

Equipment

Rockman portable headphone amplifier, designed by Tom Scholz, of the group Boston.

Circa 1965 Fender Deluxe-Reverb.

amount of distortion you require at various volumes. Some amps have two separate channels, which can be set for different sounds. It's important that the amp have a footswitch of some kind to activate this channel-switching when needed.

The features can keep piling up, depending on how much you're willing to spend. The ones that I have mentioned represent what I feel are the bare essentials for having a small amp that works for your best interest, while not leaving you broke.

Large Amplifiers

For anyone interested in heavy metal guitar, the large amplifier is probably a favorite subject. It's like the owner of a Corvette talking about the engine, or a truck driver talking about his rig. It's a fact: heavy metal is based on *powerful* amplification!

For many years, the trend for guitarists and bass players has been to use multiples of amps, or "stacks," as to get the true "wall-of-sound" effect. This began back in the 1960s with groups like The Who, Blue Cheer, and Led Zeppelin leading the way with Marshalls, Hiwatts, Voxes, or whatever else they could get to stack up behind them. This established the British amp as reigning supreme in the world of heavy metal. With the exception of a few American manufacturers who are making some excellent large and powerful amps, such as Seymour Duncan Amps and Peavey, British amps continue to dominate the market.

Equipment

The "Marshall sound" has become a major component of heavy metal music, and the many stacks of amps connected together in line seems to be a metal tradition. Speaker cabinets containing four 12-inch speakers are a normal part of this setup, and many manufacturers these days are making 4 × 12 cabinets to satisfy this need. Currently, an English-made amp that is doing very well is the KMD. These amps combine both solid-state and tube electronics for an extremely good sounding and reliable product. I have personally found these amps to be excellent, and they are also a terrific buy amidst today's high prices.

The KMD—a fine British-made amp for the heavy metal sound.

Marshall, Ampeg, Hiwatt, Yamaha, and Peavey are all fine names when it comes to heavy metal equipment, and many of them produce amps that are solid-state or tube or both. There is no doubt in my mind that tube amps sound superior. The tubes have a much more natural resonance, and the guitar's "true colors" can sound forth. However, tube amps are more delicate and their circuitry makes them more susceptible to shock and impact, particularly on the road. All-transistor amplifiers tend to have a "compressed" sound, with a lot of mid-range and not enough true bass or treble response, but they *do* tend to be a bit more reliable. Amps that combine a transistor pre-amp with a tube power amp such as the KMD give you the best of both worlds, and are highly recommended under today's performing and recording conditions. A 100-watt "head" or amplifier section, with one or two speaker cabinets or "bottoms" containing four 12-inch speakers, should be fine for you.

For the person with more cash to put down, there are some superb "exotic" amps on the market today that are state of the art when it comes to all-tube technology. Makers such as Howard Dumble, Seymour Duncan, Jim Kelly, and Mesa Boogie have developed high-status reputations for exclusive hand-built amps. They all make various configurations, including separate head-and-bottom setups. It's important to keep in mind that while these amps are finely crafted and in many cases deliver better sound, they *are* more fragile, and tend not to hold up well under the rigors of the road.

Seymour Duncan double-stack amp.

Equipment

EFFECTS BOXES

Delay, chorus, phase-shifters, and flangers have become regular parts of the modern musician's vocabulary, and all are almost necessary to have in one's arsenal of sounds. For a long time, heavy metal didn't incorporate much more than some echo for effect, but these days, the more sophisticated pieces of equipment have become part of the standard setup used by heavy metal's biggest stars.

Most of the effects one would need are available in foot pedal form, though many of today's players prefer the more sophisticated (and expensive) rack-mounted digital units. The rack-mounted setups usually offer more versatility and flexibility, but the simple floor-mounted pedals are certainly good enough for any application I can imagine and they are very *convenient!* Their portability makes them a great asset in studio work as well, where you must be prepared to create almost any sound needed on the spur of the moment.

Perhaps the effect most often used is the **delay unit.** With this device we can make our notes *repeat*, creating a sense of space and distance. Be sure to buy a delay that enables you to control how many times the repeat occurs, how long each repeat is, *and* how loud the repeats are in relation to the original note. These features are on just about every unit available these days, and they give you a great deal of creative flexibility. In the case of digital delays (which I recommend over the older analog type), it seems that the more expensive the unit, the longer the delay possibility. Long, extended echoes are very desirable, especially when trying to get that really "big" stadium-like sound. For this reason, I recommend that you try to purchase a delay unit that allows you as long a delay as possible. It always seems that one wants to be able to create longer and longer delays in one's playing, while the shorter delays are usually adequately covered by all units.

An assortment of effects boxes.

The **chorus unit** has gained an incredible amount of popularity of late. I call it the "effect of the 1980s" because it has been so prevalent during the last ten years, not only on guitar, but on bass and keyboards as well. The chorus creates an almost "doubled" effect on an instrument by adding a second, slightly wavering duplicate of the original pitch. This wavering can be adjusted to enable you to have either a very elegant, bell-like slow chorus, or a quickly quivering-type of chorus sound. It's almost as if you're playing two strings together, one only slightly out of pitch to the other. One problem with chorusing is that it's such a pretty sound that you can get spoiled by it, and have a hard time accepting your normal sound once you return to it! An amazingly versatile sound, it's as at home on a heavy metal tune played on full volume through a stack of Marshalls as it is on an acoustic guitar while fingerpicking a country song. I strongly recommend owning a chorus unit, and there are many small pedal models that give great sound quality for the money. They are guaranteed to give you years of musical pleasure!

Phase shifters were first popularized in the early to mid–1970s—so much so that it's almost possible to date a record by its presence! They are still around, but the chorus unit has certainly overtaken it in popularity. The phaser creates the same effect as the revolving Leslie speaker unit utilized by organ players. This creates a "sweep" of sound that recreates the "pealing" of the organ. This is, of course, in the slow setting. You can speed up the oscillation to make for some very warbled effects, many of which were used on the records of the disco era. Even though the chorus unit is more popular and an arguably prettier sound, I still recommend owning a phase unit for those moments when no other sound effect will do.

The **flanger** is also an older effect, but one that is still important to the sound of many guitarists. Like the phaser, it creates some sweeping sounds that utilize shifts in tonality as a basis for its effect. The flanger is definitely a more extreme sounding effect than the phaser or chorus, and it's not for everyone. I would recommend trying one out and seeing if it really fits into the way you see yourself playing the guitar and the kinds of sounds you wish to make. I'm of the opinion that if you already have a phaser and chorus, a flanger would just be excess baggage.

Wah-wah pedals, those rock and roll icons of late-1960s psychedelia, are making a comeback in today's music. The 1960s are back with a vengeance, given that the wah-wah was frequently used by guitar heroes of the 1960s such as Jimi Hendrix (the king of the wah-wah), Jeff Beck, and Eric Clapton. What's interesting (and also refreshing) about this unit is that you have physical control over how it affects the notes you choose. This is because it's a pedal with an up-and-down movement that you can synchronize with the notes you are playing, making it a natural extension of the act of playing the guitar. The sound of the wah-wah is sort of like its name. You open and close the tonal range of the note as you raise and lower the pedal. To understand this kind of sound, play a note and turn the tone control of the guitar off and on. This makes the note go from a clear sound to a muffled sound and back, hence the "wah" in the effect. Players such as Steve Vai and others are making great use of this long–ignored and intriguing device.

Overdrive units are also quite popular these days, and many of them

Equipment

very accurately replicate the sound of a naturally overdriven amp or speaker. This is particularly useful if you are working with a small amp setup, for you cannot only get more distortion, but more volume as well—two characteristics quite important to heavy metal playing! I highly recommend using overdrive units especially in a very loud group situation, where your loudest just isn't enough to cut through during your solos.

This should provide you with a good cross section of the more important effects available on the market today. Try them out, and by all means enjoy them. Be sure to remember that an effect must not dominate your playing. It should be thought of as a tool in the hands of a creative individual who knows just when to use it. Don't let yourself become one of those guitarist who always "falls back" on effects to compensate for a general lack of inventiveness that can be achieved with two hands, a guitar, and an amp!

Reading Tablature, Symbols, and Standard Notation

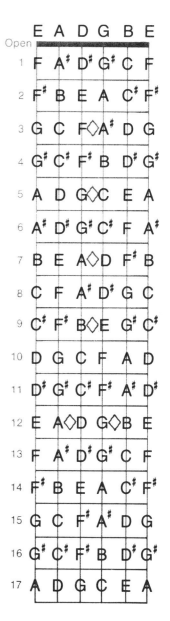

Learning to read music well is, for some, a lifelong venture. It takes incredible amounts of practice and discipline, and is often not achieved by many musicians. Because the guitar is an instrument that is so easily "picked up" by ear, its players are perhaps the least likely of all musicians to read music. This is not to say that reading music isn't important, however, for it can open doors to new pieces of music. The study necessary to make you a truly great reader would easily require another book, so for the most part, we'll stick to the basics. First, here are the notes, and how they appear on the fingerboard.

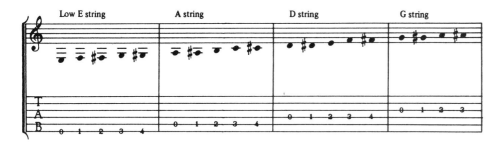

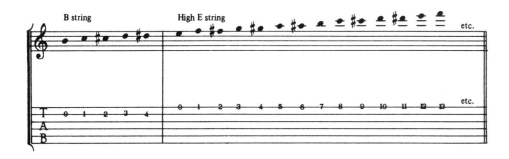

Reading Tablature, Symbols, and Standard Notation

RHYTHMIC NOTATION

How long or short we play a note is called its *time value*, and is, of course, essential to the phrasing of musical passages. In this book, and in much of western music, the measures are played in four/quarter, or 4/4 time. This simply means that there are four beats to the measure, and that each is of a one quarter note time value. Here, we see the measure with four even quarter notes.

A half note is called so because it consists of two quarter notes, dividing the 4/4 measure in half.

A whole note has no stem, and its time value consists of all four quarter notes.

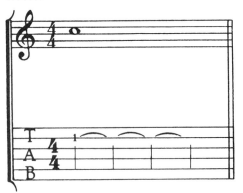

Measures can also be broken up into eighth notes, each getting half the value of a quarter note.

When we play triplets, we are dividing up the 4/4 measure into four groups of 3, or 12 notes all together. This type of rhythmic figure is sometimes written as 12/8 time, and there is usually a *3* with an arch over each group of triplets.

This type of even division is fairly endless, and there are sixteenth, thirty-second, and even sixty-fourth notes.

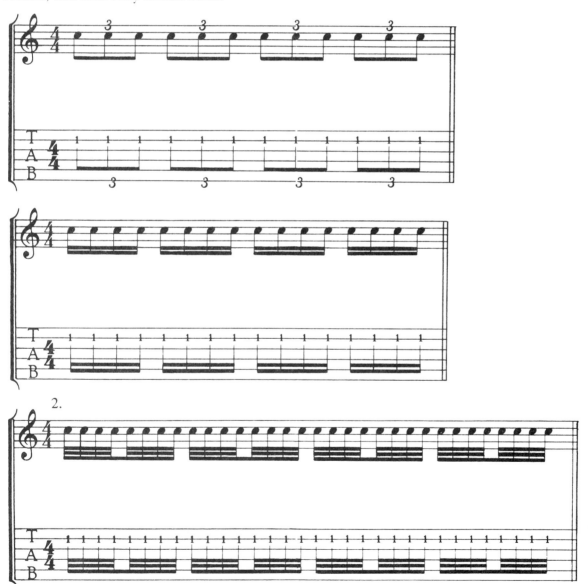

Reading Tablature, Symbols, and Standard Notation

A dotted note receives an extra half of its time value. This is how we would represent a note that receives three quarter notes worth of time value.

Here we see how the "triplet" feel can be created with dotted eighth notes. This is the well-known shuffle approach to blues and jazz playing.

We can also indicate a note's time extension by the use of *ties*. When the note is tied to an additional note of the same pitch, it receives that additional time value. To see some of the various possibilities, study the next diagram carefully.

Reading Tablature, Symbols, and Standard Notation

Rests indicate periods where we don't play; they also have time values. Here is how they're written for the various durations, and how they'll appear in the tablature as well.

In this diagram, we see how the various rhythmic values of both the notes and the rests can be put together. As a practice, try *tapping* out the rhythms with your hand while maintaining the four/quarter (4/4) beat in your head. Try to keep it going, even if you make a mistake.

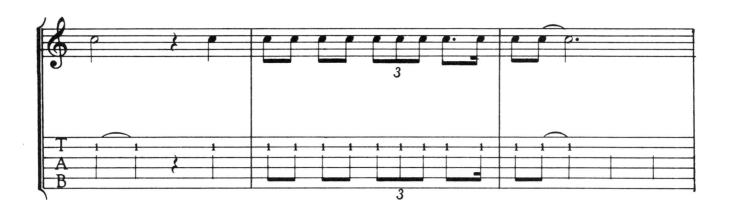

TABLATURE

For those who cannot read music, and for those who can and would like an additional aid, I've provided guitar tablature below all of the standard notation in this book. Tablature consists simply of six horizontal lines, representing the six strings of the guitar, with the high E string at the top.

Any number intersecting a line (string) represents the number fret at which we depress that given string. For example, this is how we would represent an open C chord in tablature form below the music.

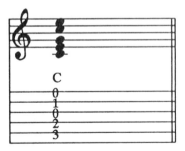

SYMBOLS

Throughout this book, I will call upon special symbols to represent certain guitar techniques. These will appear in both the tablature and standard notation.

An arch between two notes with an "S" over it indicates that you **slide** between those notes.

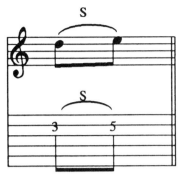

The same arch with an "H" over it indicates a **hammer-on** between those two notes. In this case, the first note is played with the pick, while the second is created solely with the finger that is "hammering-on" and fretting it higher up on the fingerboard.

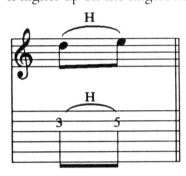

An arch with a "P" over it means that there is a **pull-off** between the notes. The second note is sounded by a downward "pluck" off of the first note, created by the fretting hand. This technique often immediately follows a hammer-on.

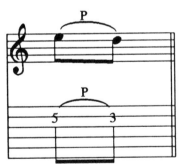

A **bend** is indicated by a "B" over the arch. When bending a note, you can raise its pitch by staying on the same fret, and then either pushing or pulling the string. In this case, the first note is bent, making it sound like the second note. Hence the use of parenthesis around the second note.

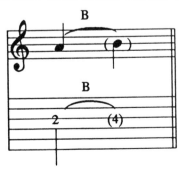

Reading Tablature, Symbols, and Standard Notation

An "R" indicates the **release** of a bend, usually following a bend.

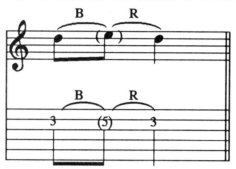

There are times when the release occurs alone, that is, the note is already bent up to pitch *before* the release occurs.

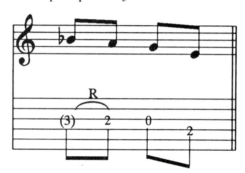

A straight line pointing up or down *toward* a note means you slide *to* that note from a point approximately two or three frets below or above it. This same line pointing *away* from the note suggests a slide *after* the note is sounded.

If the note is played with **vibrato,** there will be a wavy line over it. We'll discuss proper vibrato technique later. This same symbol will also indicate the use of the guitar's vibrato arm.

Reading Tablature, Symbols, and Standard Notation

Tapping is a very popular heavy metal technique and will be discussed at great length in this book. Tapping involves the right hand creating the note by directly tapping the note on the fretboard, abandoning the use of the pick. This is indicated by a "T" placed directly over the tapped note. This technique is often used just prior to pull-offs, as indicated in this example.

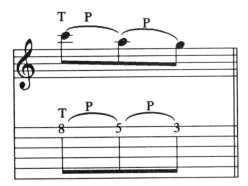

A circle (°) directly over a note indicates that the note is actually a **harmonic.** This technique requires the reading of both tablature *and* standard notation, as the fret and the note of a harmonic are not always the same. A harmonic is a bell-like chime that can be achieved by lightly touching a string

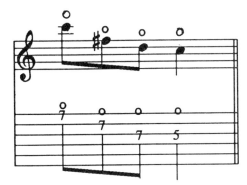

directly over a given mathematical point on the guitar. The string should be released as soon as the note is plucked for best results. There are countless points along the strings that can result in harmonics, but the strongest and most convenient are the fifth, seventh, and twelfth frets.

Fundamentals of Heavy Metal Technique

THE RIGHT HAND

Heavy metal guitar is a style that is particularly demanding on both hands. One must be able to play the most static of "power" chords, yet be able to shift immediately into fluid, rapid-fire, single-note explosions. This requires a

A relaxed position for the right hand.

Fundamentals of Heavy Metal Technique

relaxed picking hand, always ready to make sudden changes. A right hand that is too rigid will not be able to produce the fluid, rapid passages required of a lead guitarist. The photo below illustrates a good relaxed position for the picking hand. Note how the hand is not anchored—rather, it's almost "floating" above the strings, ready to fly across them for fast playing.

THE LEFT HAND

The position you assume with your left, or fretting hand, depends largely on the size of your hand and the type of playing you like to do. When executing many slow, expressive techniques such as bending strings or vibrato, I prefer

The left-hand "rock" position. Strings should intercept the fingertips at a 45° angle.

"Classical" position for the left hand. Note how the fingers touch the strings at a different angle than in the "rock" position.

Fundamentals of Heavy Metal Technique

the angled "rock" position. The longer your fingers are, the more often this position can be used. Today, the over-the-fingerboard "classical" position is the most popular for heavy metal lead playing. It is more adaptable for the four-fingered style that is often required for these elaborate runs. Here are two photos, one of the angled "rock" position, and the other of the "classical" approach. The difference in fingering is obvious, but also note how differently the thumb is positioned in both cases. The rock position enables the thumb to reach over the edge of the fretboard for extra leverage, while in the classical position it must remain behind the neck, allowing the fingers to achieve the required height.

EXERCISES FOR DEVELOPING RIGHT AND LEFT HAND COORDINATION

Chromatic runs are very useful in developing a fast technique for heavy metal playing and, in fact, you'll find that many of the licks we'll be working with in this book utilize some aspect of the chromatic approach. A chromatic run is simply a group of notes that follow in half-step groupings, never skipping a fret. These runs can be connected string-to-string, creating some very dramatic effects and some extremely flashy heavy metal licks.

To help build up your right and left hand coordination, I've written out a chromatic scale exercise for you. Your goal should be to play each note at an even tempo and volume, using constantly alternating up-and-down picking strokes. Once this is accomplished, you can build up your speed.

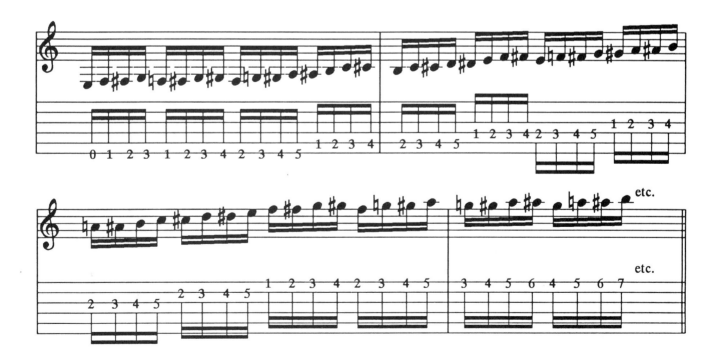

Fundamentals of Heavy Metal Technique

This next piece is one that Jay Jay French of Twisted Sister showed me. He calls it the "power warm-up," and it certainly is! It involves a simple four-fingered chromatic walk-up and walk-down on each string which helps to build strength in your alternating picking strokes as well as in all four fretting fingers. Remember, start slowly at first and build your speed as your confidence grows. Believe me, you'll be playing this piece fast in no time if you practice it enough!

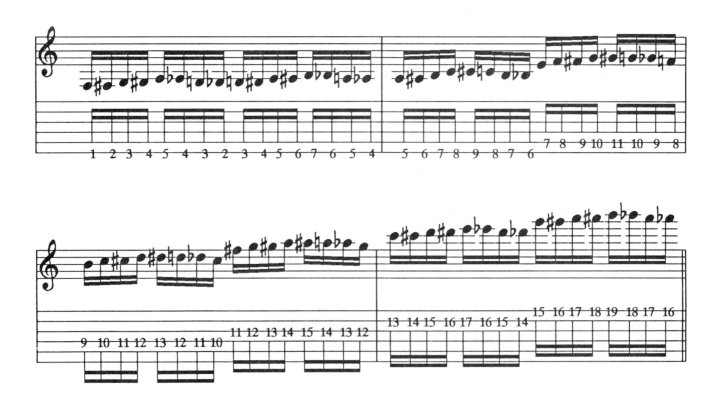

This last exercise is quite a bit trickier, and may well be left alone until later if you don't feel quite up to it yet. It's designed to help the independence of the fingers on the left hand by alternating two fingers at a time on each string. For example, you start by playing with the first and third fingers on the first and third frets of the low E string, then you switch to playing the second and fourth frets on the A string with the second and fourth fingers! This definitely comes easier to some than others, and it will take serious practice. Gradually try to play it fast, but you should be pleased with *any* progress you make! Again, be sure to use all down-up strokes, but be aware that the strings are changing more rapidly now.

Fundamentals of Heavy Metal Technique

Author Arlen Roth and Jay Jay French of Twisted Sister jamming together.
Photo: Deborah Roth.

Fundamentals of Heavy Metal Technique

STRETCHES FOR THE FOURTH FINGER

There are a lot of blues and rock players who get by with hardly ever using their pinky, but in today's heavy metal sound it's truly a finger of necessity! The ability to stretch the hand properly to utilize the fourth finger is developed only through hard work and frequent playing. Below is an exercise designed specifically with this development in mind, especially in the case of a succession of notes played by the index and the fourth fingers. These two fingers are the farthest away from each other, so the hand will benefit greatly from any exercise that concentrates on them. Keep in mind that when the pinky is fretting the note, the other finger lifts off its fret and the hand shifts slightly to accommodate the fourth finger. This is achieved by keeping the thumb anchored behind the neck so the pivoting motion can occur gracefully.

Left-hand "stretch."

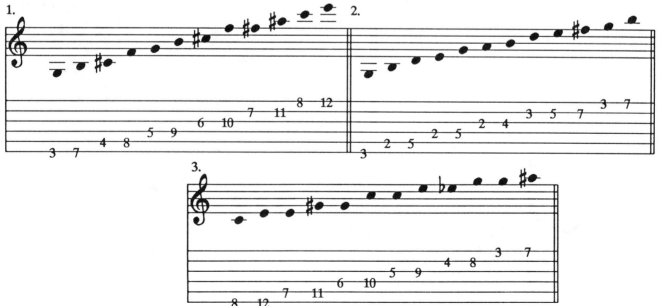

BASIC BLUES/ROCK SCALES

Much of lead rock guitar is based upon the pentatonic scales. These are most noticeable within the blues and country forms, but many of heavy metal's flashiest licks and runs are based upon these simple five-note scales. As a further aid in stretching out your hand and working your fingers, I've provided the scales in their most basic forms below. I would recommend playing these in both the rock and classical positions. While in the rock position, use and alternate between the first and *third* fingers for the big stretches, and in the classical position, use the first and *fourth* fingers. Practice these with an alternating picking stroke, and practice them frequently because these scales will be the basis for much of the work we will cover later in this book.

Fundamentals of Heavy Metal Technique

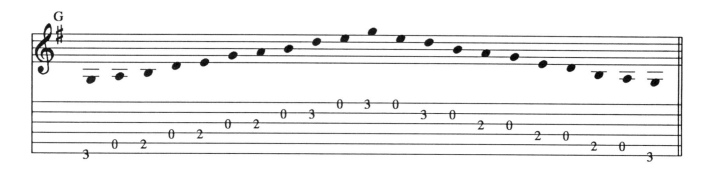

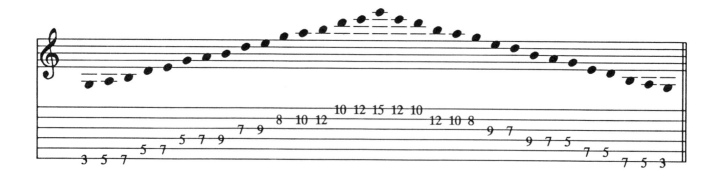

SLIDING BETWEEN NOTES

This will be your first technique for the left hand beyond simply fretting. Stylistic approaches, such as sliding between notes, bending strings, and hammer-ons and pull-offs (defined later), are what give lead guitar its true character and expression. These are the techniques that give string instruments a unique quality.

When sliding between notes, one is sounding a second note by moving to another fret after the first note has been sounded. In effect, two notes are created with one picking stroke. This requires a strong left hand technique since the finger must keep enough pressure on the string to hold its sustain long enough for the slide to create the second note. A good way of introducing this technique is to use it within the context of a scale. By doing so you can see its additional quality of enabling you to shift positions smoothly. Below is an example of sliding between notes in the appropriate context of a blues rock pentatonic scale. Note how the slide occurs three times, at three different octaves of the same two notes.

Now we see the slides in the context of a country pentatonic scale. Although it still occurs in three positions, this time it is being used for a decidedly more "major" sound than the blues pentatonic scale. Later we will see how these slides are the basis for many other techniques such as bending, hammer-ons, and pull-offs.

Be sure to practice these scales over and over until a fluidity is achieved. You'll then be able to move on to the next section which deals more directly with the foundations of heavy metal lead guitar.

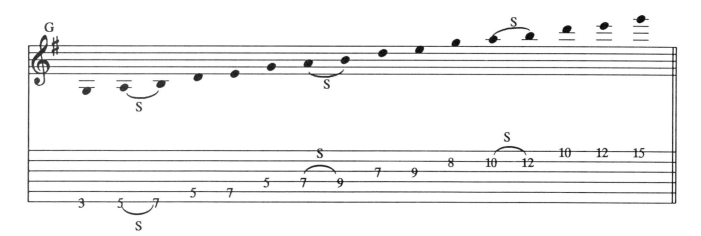

The Influence of Early Rock and Blues

Before we continue to discuss heavy metal playing per se, I think it would be beneficial for us to take a look at some of the earlier styles, which are the foundation that today's guitar styles were built upon. To know the history of your art form is very important. The early blues and rock players are all directly responsible for what is played today in heavy metal. It's like a long, connected chain: B.B. King listened to Robert Johnson, Eric Clapton listened to B.B. King, Eddie Van Halen listened to Eric Clapton, and on and on. It's for this reason that you must never underestimate the influence and importance of the earlier styles. Today there are many players who think that the guitar begins and ends with their favorite current-day hero. To think this way is definitely not wise, although very often people are introduced to the guitar as a result of a guitar hero. For instance, even though I was already playing classical guitar in 1964, I know I wouldn't have gotten an electric guitar so fast had the Beatles not shown up!

SHUFFLE PATTERNS

In the mid–1950s, such players as Chuck Berry, Jimmy Reed, and Bo Diddley created a blues-based rock 'n' roll guitar style that was to electrify music forever. Hard-driving "shuffle" rhythms, double-note licks, and aggressive sounding bends came through the radios and jukeboxes of the world, keeping in perfect step with the restless, changing times in the United States. When one thinks of early rock 'n' roll guitar styles, the "shuffle" rhythm is usually at the top of the list. This sound is as hot today as when Chuck Berry first recorded it, and the positions used for it are the basis of many of the heavy metal power chords we hear so often.

Most shuffle guitar patterns require only two notes of a chord: the root and the fifth. Since it does not require a full chord, and the notes involved are usually the two lowest of the chord, shuffle patterns are quite easy to play.

The Influence of Early Rock and Blues

The following shuffle exercise clearly illustrates this point. We use the open positions of A, D, and E—each chord with its root and fifth at the bottom. In each case, the fretted part of the chord is played by the index finger and the note that is alternated to above the chord is played by the third finger. If this feels like too much of a stretch for you, use your pinky for now. It's important to note that left hand "damping" is crucial here, as we want only two strings to ring at a time. The photo below shows my fingers playing the beginning of the shuffle lick. Notice that my thumb is curled slightly over the fingerboard to stop the low E string from ringing, while the remainder of my index finger lightly touches the rest of the strings, effectively damping out any unwanted overtones. Try to keep your picking very accurate and contained to two strings. Don't completely rely upon left-hand damping to the point of weakening your right-hand technique! Play this piece with all *downstrokes* to enhance its aggressive attack and sound.

Open A power chord position.

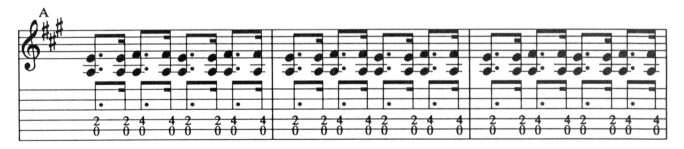

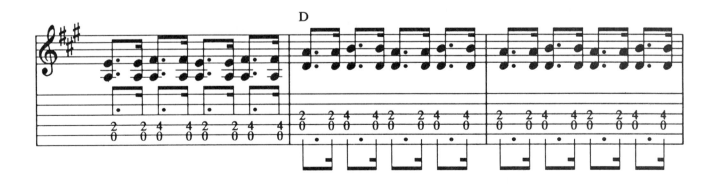

The Influence of Early Rock and Blues

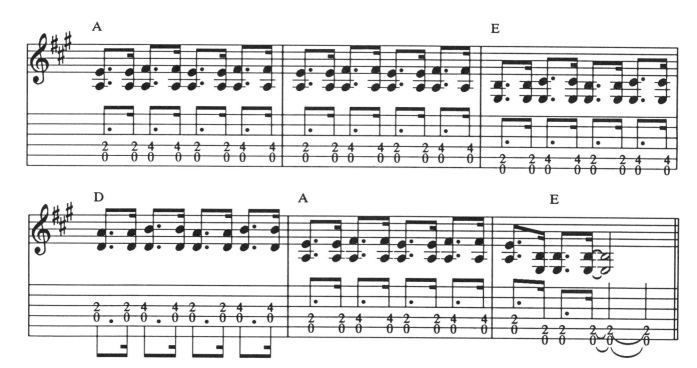

Chuck Berry.
© Ebet Roberts, 1983.

The Influence of Early Rock and Blues

Start of "closed" shuffle position.

In this shuffle pattern, the two bottom-most notes of the barre-form chords are used. Since we don't have the luxury of open strings, these patterns require more effort. The bottom note must be anchored while the other part of the chord alternates. Again, the index finger presses down on the lower string, while it lays lightly across the remaining strings to damp out other tones.

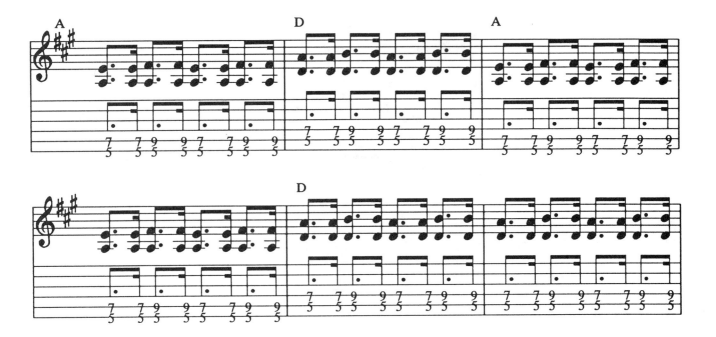

▲ 45

The Influence of Early Rock and Blues

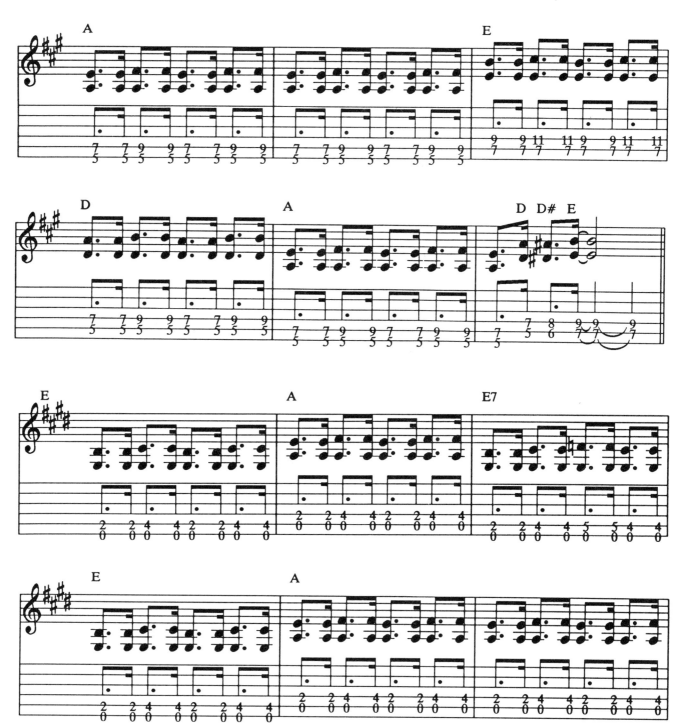

Sometimes we must combine open and closed positions for this kind of lick, as in the following exercise for E. This is particularly tricky, for it involves easy open position shuffles, but then suddenly shifts to a closed form of B that exists where the frets are the widest. This makes for a rather extreme stretch that may be a bit too much for you at this time. Try it and see how ready you are—at least it'll be a good stretching exercise!

The Influence of Early Rock and Blues

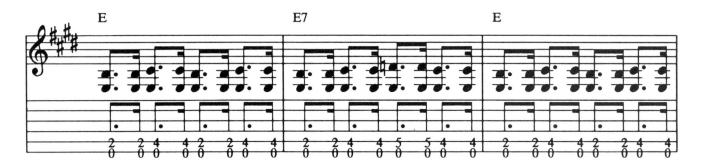

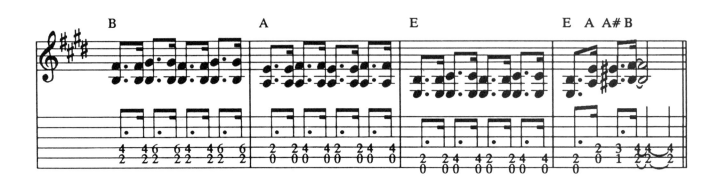

Blues and rock stars such as B.B. King and Eric Clapton have had a profound effect on the evolution of the guitar. Others have played important roles as well, such as Mike Bloomfield, Otis Rush, T Bone Walker, Freddie King, Albert King, and Lonnie Mack. These players were all listened to and emulated by many of the "heavier" players of the 1960s, 1970s, and 1980s. As I stated earlier, Eddie Van Halen, the reigning king of heavy metal guitar, learned a great deal by listening to Clapton while growing up, even though their respective styles couldn't be more different.

Much of the playing for which these players are known is based both on the minor (blues) pentatonic scale positions as well as on the more major (country-like) pentatonic scales. As a quick way to get you involved in this kind of playing, I've broken the lesson down to each scale and its respective licks, so you can get used to playing within certain positions. However, before we continue, it's crucial that we take a look at another extremely important and expressive technique for the lead guitarist: string bending.

The Influence of Early Rock and Blues

STRING BENDING

In my opinion this technique is unique to guitar playing, and gives guitar an extra measure of appeal rarely found in other instruments. The ability to "bend" a string to a different tone gives the guitarist power over just which note he or she wants to express, and keeps all of that expressiveness at the touch of a finger. The physical act of string bending is often a misunderstood technique. I've had students come to me who have been playing for fifteen years but still don't know anything about proper string bending.

The crucial thing to keep in mind is that, in general, to bend strings properly you need the help of extra fingers. This widens the point at which the string is pulled and gives the added strength necessary to sustain the note, or give it vibrato. Here is a photo of a bend on the G string that is *towards* you. Note that even though the G string is being bent mostly by the ring finger, the middle and index fingers help push it as well. The index finger also serves the very important function of pushing the lower strings out of the way so there are no unwanted accidental sounds, as when a bent string is returned to its normal position. Also take note of how the thumb curls slightly over the edge of the fingerboard, applying opposite pressure to the bend. This creates the "choke" position that many people refer to when bending strings.

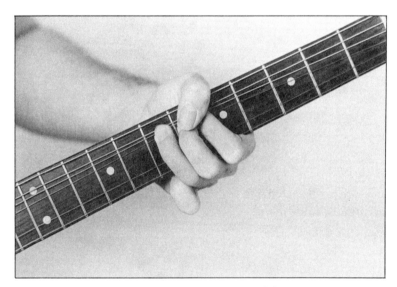

Bending the G string *towards* you, with three fingers.

Here is the same bend, only bent down, *away* from you. This involves more pivoting from the part of the hand that is against the side of the neck, but still uses as many fingers as possible to execute the bend cleanly. The decision of whether to bend a string up or down (if you have the room) is largely based on what the upcoming notes of the phrase are. For example, if you anticipate playing some notes on the B and high E strings after a bend on the G string has occurred, it would be advisable to bend the G string *towards* you.

The Influence of Early Rock and Blues

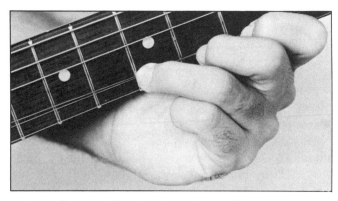

A three-fingered G-string bend *away* from you.

Here are two photos of a two-fingered bend with the middle finger leading, in both *towards* and *away* positions. In this kind of bend, the middle finger is not getting as much help as the ring finger had before, so it may have some trouble maintaining the pitch until it becomes stronger. Note how the index finger is still playing the dual roles of bend-helper and string-pusher.

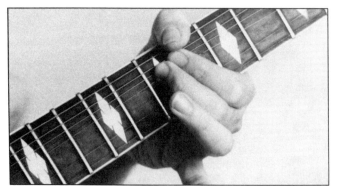 

Bending *toward* you with two fingers. **Bending *away* from you with two fingers.**

Index finger bends can be very effective and not too difficult even though that finger is doing the bend alone. For this kind of bend I would generally recommend the *pivoting* approach (as shown in the photo) because it gives you far more leverage, strength, and control.

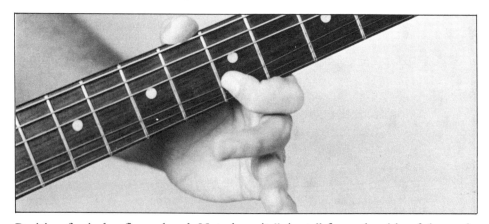

Position for index-finger bend. Note how it "pivots" from the side of the neck.

The Influence of Early Rock and Blues

There are no *wrong* notes, only notes that are played in the wrong places. This is most apparent in the case of players who are newcomers to string bending, and who have yet to train their ears to reach the proper pitch with their bends. For this reason, I've written out the following scales for you, with the notes to bend *encircled*. With each of these bends, I want you to try to bend the note up to the pitch of the note that immediately *follows*. In most cases, this will be a whole-step, or two frets, in distance. Try to maintain the bend's pitch for as long as possible without it slipping. Start this technique slowly at first, for it can be quite difficult for beginners!

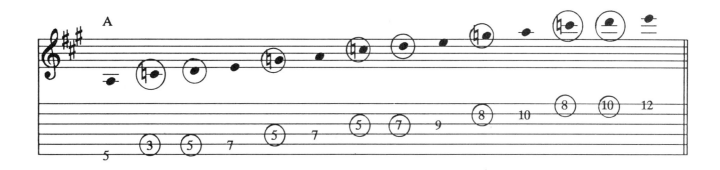

The Influence of Early Rock and Blues

Eric Clapton.
© Ebet Roberts, 1985.

The Influence of Early Rock and Blues

BLUES LICKS

Open Position Blues Licks

To begin learning some licks it would be easiest and most advisable to start off with the open position of E. This position offers easy bending and, of course, the luxury of open strings. In addition, it is a very basic form of the same blues scales we'll be using. Note that in many of these licks, we are making half-step as well as whole-step bends, and we're playing "passing tones" within the scale. These are notes that are not in the actual scale we are using, but serve to "pass" from one note to another as part of the musical phrase. In the case of a pentatonic blues scale, these passing notes are often the flatted fifth of the scale. In this scale in E, the flatted fifth is an A#.

The Influence of Early Rock and Blues

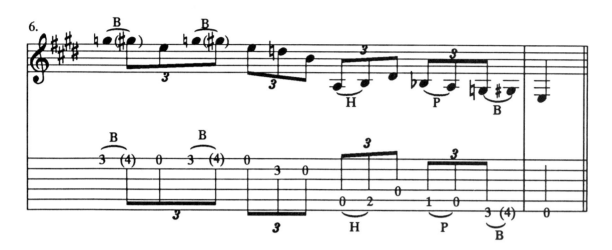

Closed Position Blues Licks (Short Scale)

Now we can move up the fingerboard to the "closed" position of this scale. You should note one specific change: the second note of the scale (in this case a C) is now played on the A string as opposed to the way we played the G on the third fret on the E string in the last scale. I believe that although you may still experiment with playing the C at the eighth fret on the low E, its position on the A string affords you many more improvisational opportunities and facilitates better movement in general.

The following runs are selected from this "closed" scale and make use of many slides and bends. You'll find them to be reminiscent of the blues playing of Eric Clapton, Mike Bloomfield, B.B. King, and other legendary masters. Remember to make these sound like *music*. Don't treat them as merely exercises, or else you will fail to develop as a musician. This goes for scales also. Far too many players end up sounding like they're merely running through the motions in a scale-like manner regardless if they're soloing or just practicing. Remember: it's fun, *not* practice!

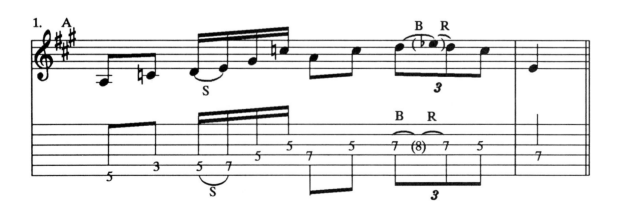

▲ 53

The Influence of Early Rock and Blues

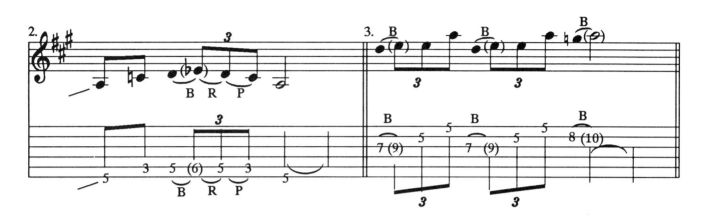

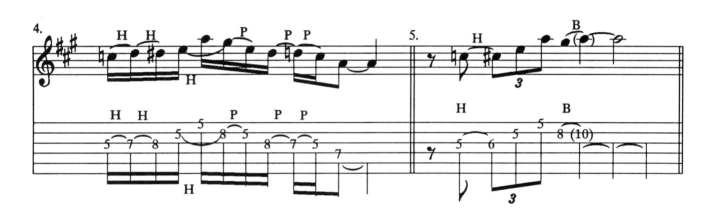

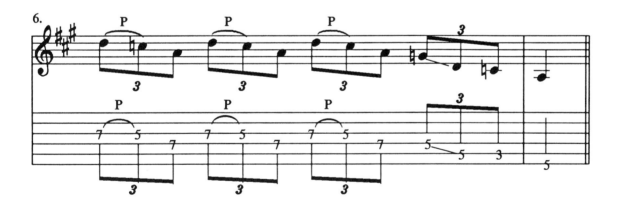

Closed Position Blues Licks (Long Scale)

This longer, more extended version of the closed pentatonic blues scale offers even further possibilities, and opens up a higher box-like position up the neck. As you'll see in the exercises that follow, there are a wealth of licks achievable with this position. Some should be recognizable to you, not only in the blues idiom, but in heavy metal as well.

The Influence of Early Rock and Blues

MAJOR PENTATONIC LICKS

Major Pentatonic Licks (Short Scale)

Our first closed position of the major pentatonic scale does more than just resemble the blues scales we've been working with. This is no coincidence, as it really *is* the same scale—only now its relationship to the chord is totally different. For example, if we want to find the minor blues pentatonic for the same key, we simply move it all up three frets or a step and a half. Conversely, the major pentatonic scale of A is also the minor blues pentatonic scale for F#, three frets below it. I know it all seems a little confusing now, but it will

The Influence of Early Rock and Blues

become clearer as you play more. Note that these licks remain within the three-fret area defined by this scale, which creates another nice "box" pattern to work within.

The Influence of Early Rock and Blues

Major Pentatonic Licks: (Long Scale)

The longest major pentatonic scale is truly a joy to work with. It enables you to cover a tremendous amount of territory in a relatively short amount of time. The first couple of licks below are more like new ways to play the scale itself than they are short musical passages. They enable you to connect the notes with even more fluidity, and serve as a great training for partial barres. A **partial barre** is when a part of your finger is used to cover two or more strings at a time on the same fret. This makes many licks and positions possible that weren't possible before, and creates the foundations for hammer-ons and pull-offs.

Near the end of the scale, we reach what I refer to as the B.B. King box position, where many of his trademark licks come from. These have a decidely country-like sound, and have been adapted by players such as Eric Clapton and Buddy Guy. Note how in these licks, a whole-step bend defines the major chord, while bending it only a half-step defines either a minor chord, or even the IV chord by becoming its minor seventh. This is a very commonly used device in the blues and rock idioms, so please take special note of these licks.

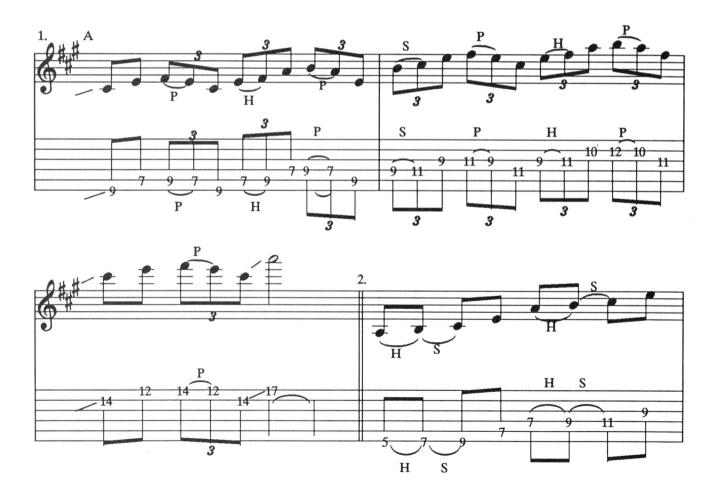

▲ 57

The Influence of Early Rock and Blues

HAMMER-ONS AND PULL-OFFS

Hammer-ons and pull-offs are true necessities for the lead or rhythm guitarist, and are very useful in chordal as well as single-note work. Put simply, the fretting hand executes a **hammer-on** which creates another note *after* the first note is plucked. This gives the guitarist the freedom to create more than one

The Influence of Early Rock and Blues

note for every stroke of the pick. The same applies to the **pull-off** which, with one exception, is the opposite of a hammer-on. While a hammer-on is created by the finger coming directly down upon the string to create the new note, a pull-off is more than just a "lift-off." In order to create a tone long enough to sustain the new note, it requires a downward "pluck" of the finger that was fretting the note.

In the following two photos, we see the act of "hammering-on" and the position of the fingers just after the pull-off, or left-hand "pluck," has occurred. Note how the finger has plucked down and *away*.

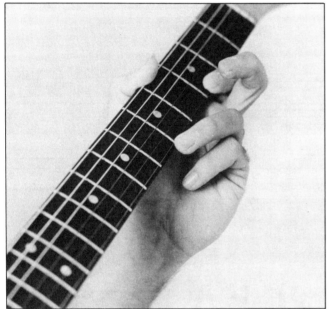
Left-hand "hammer-on" with the third finger.

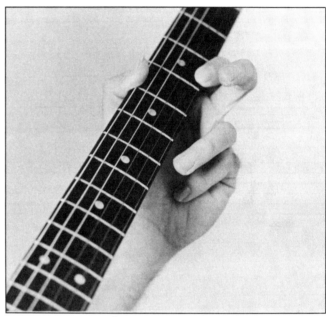
The left hand just after a third-finger "pull-off."

Here are some basic exercises to familiarize yourself with hammer-ons and pull-offs. Some are intended to be executed with the second finger, while others are hammered with either the ring or pinky. When doing pull-offs, be sure to have the lower-fret finger anchored strongly enough so the pluck doesn't pull the string out of tune. Notice that some licks have the more advanced combined usage of hammers *and* pulls in the same musical passage. These should be practiced carefully at first, making sure your hammers and pulls are accurate.

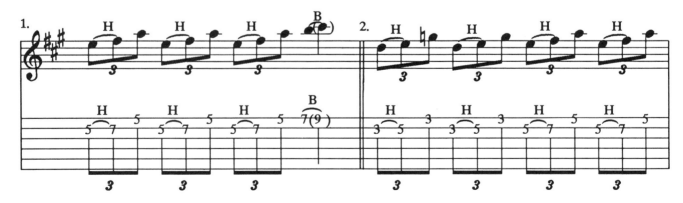

▲ 59

The Influence of Early Rock and Blues

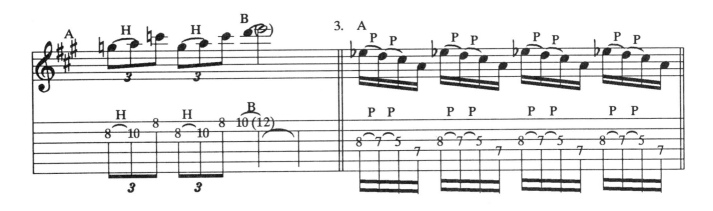

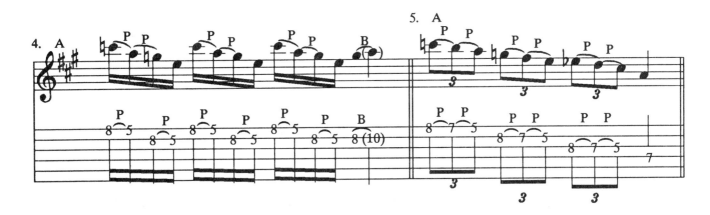

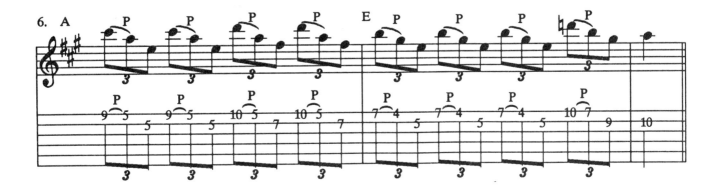

VIBRATO

No discussion of *any* style of guitar playing would be complete without thoroughly examining the art of vibrato. This technique is frequently misunderstood especially by people who have not done much "rootsy" playing, or have listened to some of the great blues and early rock players. Artists such as B.B. King, Otis Rush, Eric Clapton, and Mike Bloomfield were able to perfect a particularly sensitive form of vibrato that was as effective at low volumes as

The Influence of Early Rock and Blues

it was with the amps cranked high. This means the control of the vibrato was strong enough to sustain the string while even minute vibrations at very low volumes could be heard. This kind of vibrato was taken to much higher, heavy metal-like volumes by players such as Robin Trower (with Procol Harum), Jimi Hendrix, and Leslie West, all of whom specialized in their own brand of power vibrato.

Vibrato as a Pivoting Motion

The easiest way to become acquainted with proper vibrato technique is to understand it as a "pivoting" motion. This particular approach applies only when you're vibrato is moving *away* from you. Notice the pivoting action in the two photos that follow. My index finger creates the vibrato as the result of turning my *entire* hand approximately 15°. My hand is pivoting off of a point on the lower part of my index finger, which is pressing against the side of the neck. For the vibrato to be true, it's important that the entire hand is free in this instance. It is crucial to have the finger anchored to the side of the neck to keep the vibrato from becoming too extreme, and also allow the hand to "memorize" its original position so it can keep returning to it. The pulsation of the vibrato is created as a result of this back-and-forth pivot in a subtle bend-and-release action.

Ready to "pivot" to create vibrato.

After "pivot" has occurred.

Bending with Vibrato

There are times when we don't have the luxury of the "pivoting" position for vibrato. This is when we must vibrate a note that is bent in the direction of the low E string, or *towards* us. As shown in the photo below, a certain degree of the pivot-like position can be maintained even when we bend away. This enables us to achieve accurate vibrato without too much strain on the left hand. This is not the case in bends towards us, however, as the entire hand is committed to maintaining the pitch of the bend. This type of bend is responsible for vibrato and the desired wavering pitch is actually created by a slight and controlled release-bend-release action. This is a very difficult form of vibrato to learn and may take a great deal of time to master. The main problem

The Influence of Early Rock and Blues

is that the hand and ear are completely responsible for keeping the pitch of the bend *and* the vibrato consistent. A slight deviation from this consistency can cause catastrophic pitch and rhythm problems, probably resulting in several loud "clangs." When trying this form of vibrato, bend the string (preferably the G) up a whole-step. Once the bend has reached its pitch, start the vibrato by slowly releasing and re-bending the string a very slight—but consistent—amount. Proceed very slowly at first, for the string will probably feel like it's getting away from you, and the pitch will start to falter as a result. Note in the photo that my thumb is curled around the edge of the fingerboard, as in the normal bending position, to help the vibrato as well as the bend.

A three-fingered G-string bend *away* from you.

STARTING TO PUT IT ALL TOGETHER

Here is your chance to see how far you've come. It's still early in the book, and although we haven't really delved into heavy metal itself, all of the lead guitar skills are within your grasp! The exercises that follow provide a healthy combination of all the techniques we've discussed thus far, such as hammer-ons, pull-offs, slides between notes, string bending, and vibrato. These exercises are primarily aimed at strengthening these left-hand specialties before we move on to the more demanding heavy metal approach. Once you have a good grasp of these concepts, you will have a much better understanding of the foundations of heavy metal and there should be just the right amount of "roots" in your playing. I feel this is essential if one is to become a truly well-rounded player. After all, heavy metal is popular now, but it never was and never will be the only game in town!

I've tried to mix up these exercises, particularly by attitude and feeling. Some are bluesy, while others hint at the heavy metal approach—especially in terms of the chord progressions used. Try to see the various differences I'm attempting to get across in terms of feeling. Remember, all of these techniques are only tools to help bring out what's inside of you through music.

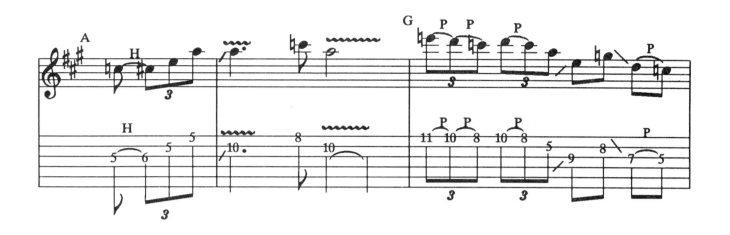
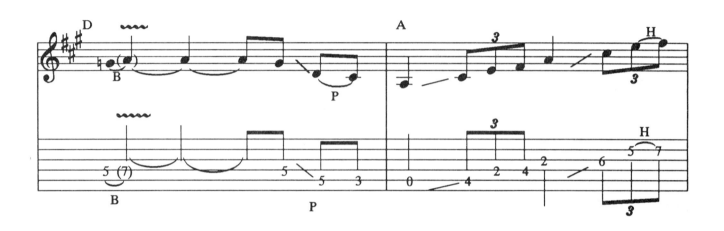
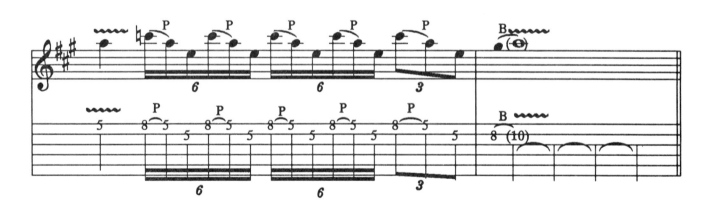
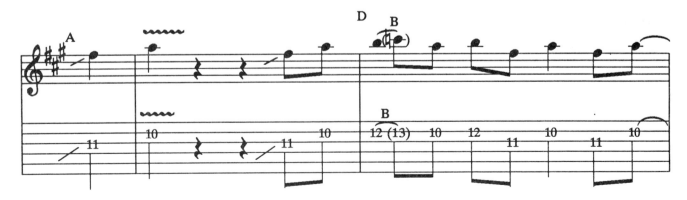

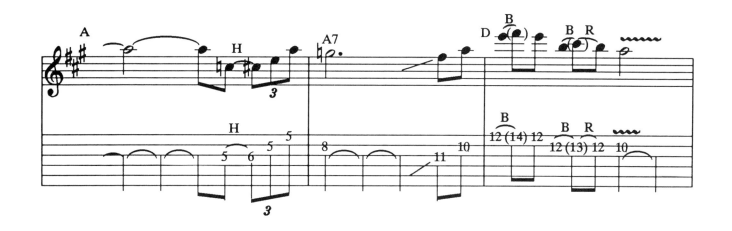
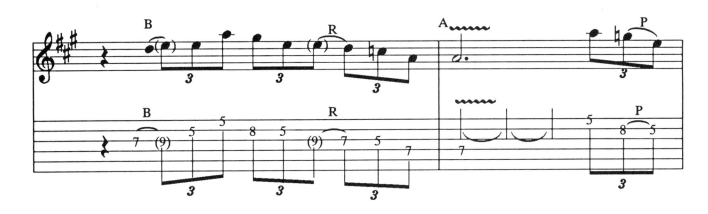
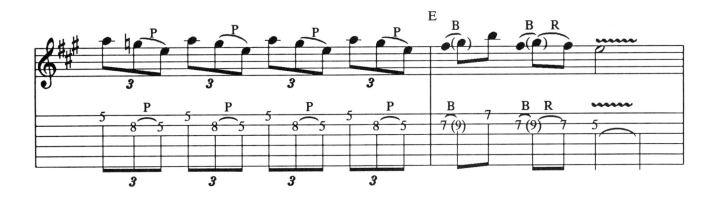
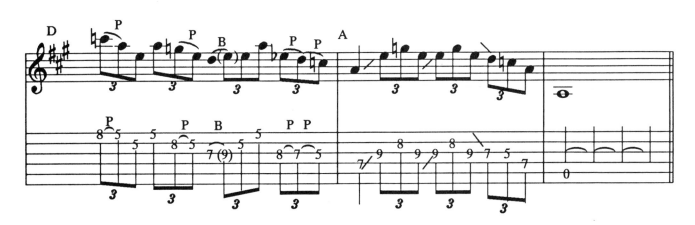

63

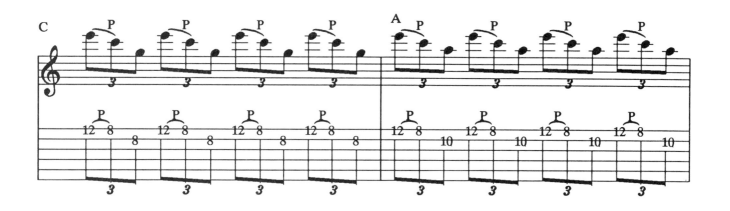
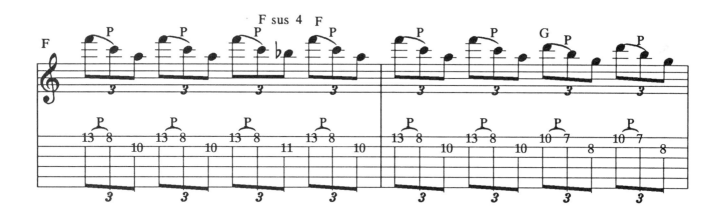
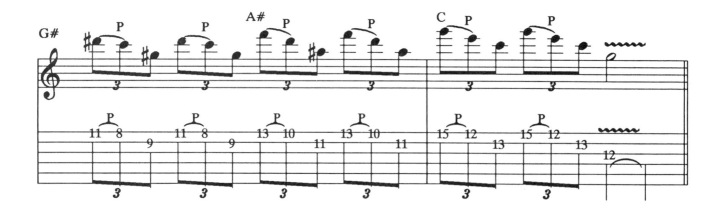

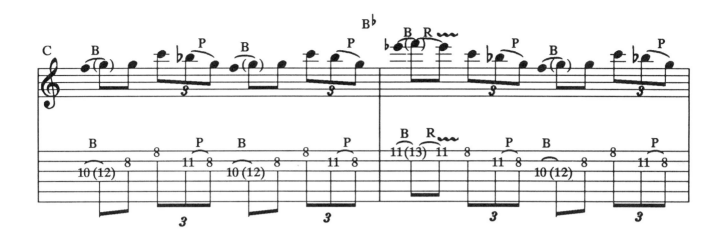
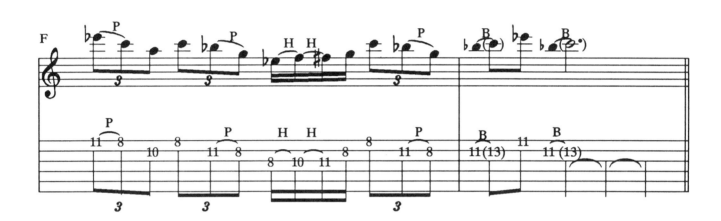

SOME BLUES GREATS

In this section, I'd like to concentrate on some of the blues guitarists who have had a profound impact on heavy metal guitar. Of course, *all* blues is at the root of the metal that we hear these days, but there is no question that some players had more influence than others.

ROBERT JOHNSON

Robert Johnson, the king of the Delta blues singers from Mississippi, recorded a group of songs in the 1930s that arguably contained more "future influence" than any work ever created. Songs such as "Dust My Broom," "Love in Vain," "Crossroads," and "Rollin' and Tumblin' " all continued to be blues standards throughout the Chicago Blues electric era, the white and English blues revivals of the 1960s, and have yet to lose their momentum. In the late 1960s and early 1970s, Cream and The Rolling Stones were the most notable bands to give widespread exposure to the songs of Robert Johnson.

In 1985, I had the good fortune to coach guitar and create all the guitar parts for actor Ralph Macchio in the movie *Crossroads*, a film based largely on the music and lore of Robert Johnson. This movie had a profound impact on today's guitar generation, and undoubtedly introduced blues to many who were only marginally aware of it before.

The author with Ralph Macchio.
Photo: Stephen Vaughan.
Courtesy Columbia Pictures.

Some Robert Johnson Licks

Johnson played in a style quite far removed from what we are familiar with in today's heavy metal, yet within his guitar parts there is an almost haunting anticipation of what *was* to come. You'll see what I mean in the following licks, played in standard tuning as opposed to the open tunings he preferred. These are rhythm guitar parts that accompanied his vocals. Note the similarity these early parts have to some "power chord" heavy metal licks.

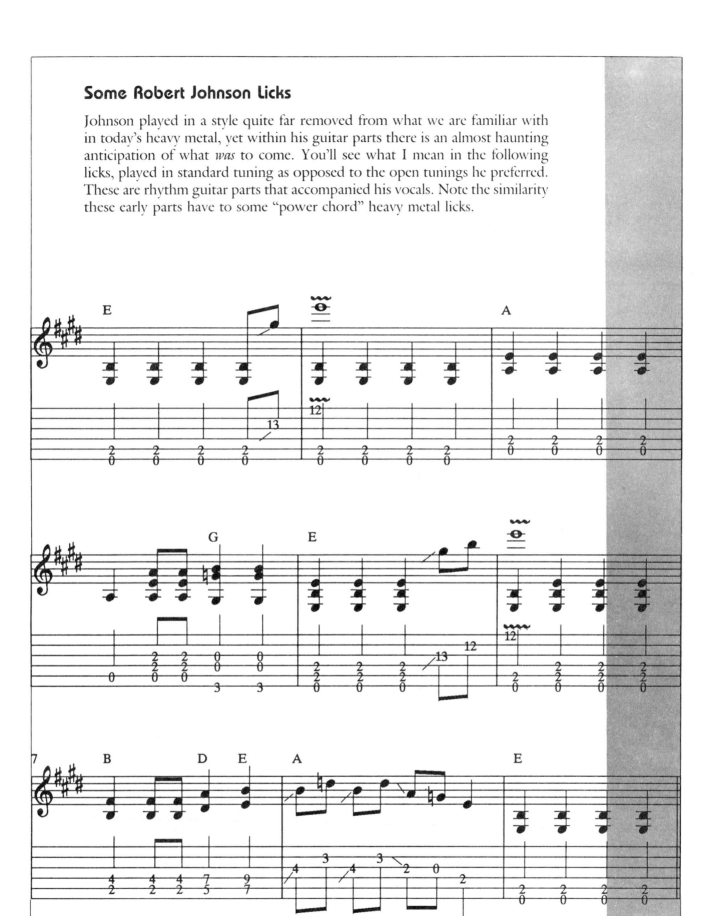

OTIS RUSH

Otis Rush is a "young generation" Chicago Blues lead guitarist who beyond blues aficionados has never gained the widespread fame he deserves. His incredible bending and vibrato power significantly influenced the playing of Eric Clapton and many others. You can never forget this man's touch on the instrument once you hear it nor can you deny the strong effect it has had on future generations of players. Here are some trademark licks in the style of Otis Rush; again, be sure to make use of the bending and strong vibrato.

Otis Rush.
© Jon Sievert, 1985.

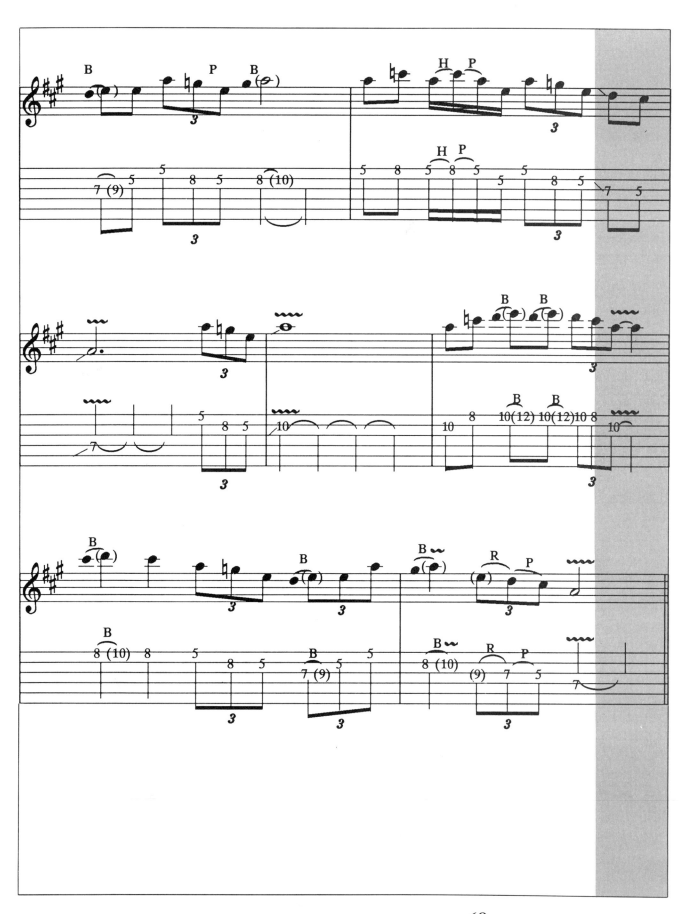

BUDDY GUY

Another comparatively young Chicago Blues artist, Buddy Guy is certainly one of the most distinctive as well as influential players of our time. Another strong influence on Eric Clapton, as well as Jimmy Page and countless others, he possesses both a fiery style and a gentler, more sensitive blues touch on the instrument. He has made several solo blues albums, and has also done some wonderful work with harmonica-great Junior Wells. The following guitar phrases embody some of Buddy Guy's most imaginative sounds. Note his unique use of continuous harmony notes within a lick; something that seems more piano-like than guitar-oriented.

Buddy Guy.
© Jon Sievert, 1987.

71

B.B. KING

A household name when it comes to the blues, B.B. King is a musical giant who has affected almost every guitar player's style at one time or another. He possesses one of the most recognizable guitar styles under the sun. His phrasing, tone, and vibrato have influenced an entire generation of players. He certainly deserves to be called the "King of Blues Guitar."

B.B. (Blues Boy) King's melodic approach is so recognizable due in large part to this strong use of the major pentatonic scale. This gives his blues a bit more of an "up" feeling, with a positive sound to it, as opposed to the more mournful minor pentatonic sound. He particularly likes to stay within what I've come to refer to as the "B.B. King Box Position." This incorporates a very small area of the fingerboard, but he can get an unbelievable amount of licks and ideas from it. The group of licks that follow show some of his true trademark "Box" position licks, and if you're into B.B. King at all, these will certainly ring a bell. Make sure to commit your whole hand to the bending process, and to watch the intonation of your bends.

B.B. King.
© Jon Sievert, 1989.

MIKE BLOOMFIELD

I first heard Mike Bloomfield's playing on Bob Dylan's *Bringing It All Back Home* and *Highway 61* albums, and the landmark first Paul Butterfield Blues Band record. His searing, emotional lead style made him the first influential white electric blues guitarist, and his effect was immediately felt overseas where a new crop of British guitar greats were starting to develop.

Around 1966, I was deeply influenced and inspired by the fantastic guitar playing of Mike Bloomfield. His unique and sensitive vibrato, bending, and phrasing left an indelible mark on my style for years to come.

In the licks below, I've tried to capture Bloomfield's unique sound for you. His phrasing at the time was a youthful and energetic way of approaching the blues, and certainly played a big role in developing the sounds we hear today.

Mike Bloomfield.
© Jon Sievert, 1989.

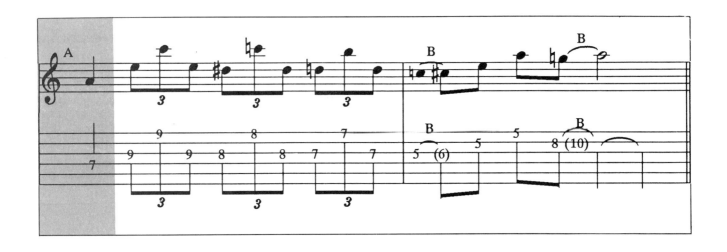

Early Heavy Metal Rhythm Guitar

Heavy metal has become a genre so dominated by lead guitar that the art of rhythm guitar has been almost totally lost. However, early heavy metal players left behind a solid legacy of rhythm techniques since this style was quite important to the metal sounds of the late 1960s and early 1970s.

POWER CHORDS

Since it was a direct outgrowth of the blues, most early heavy metal chord work was based upon the partial chords found in blues "shuffle" patterns. These seldom contain the third of the chord, but rather consist of the root and the fifth. These two "fat" sounding notes are the basis for what has become known as the "power chord" sound in heavy metal and rock guitar, and can become an easy, yet very effective method of devising interesting rhythm guitar parts within a band context.

On page 78 is a grouping of these heavy metal power chord positions in both photographic and musical forms. They correspond with the shuffle positions illustrated in the section on early rock and blues guitar. Again, use the remainder of the barreing index finger to dampen the higher strings.

POWER CHORD PROGRESSIONS

During heavy metal's rise to popular status, certain progressions became frequently used. These took the shape of countless songs, and many times were only part of the overall piece of music. Power chord parts were often played in conjunction with the bass player, further accentuating the heaviness of the bass lines. This is why many power chord applications are more staccato than legato, adding to the "punch" and fatness of the sound.

Early Heavy Metal Rhythm Guitar

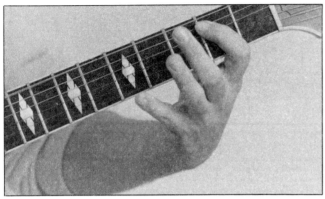

Open E power chord position.   Open A power chord position.

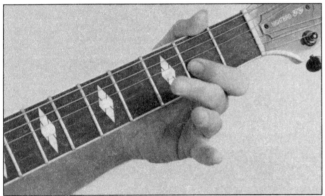

Open D power chord position.   G power chord position.

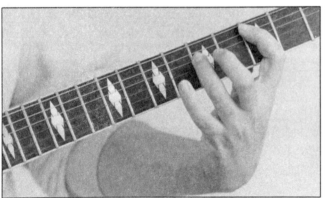

C power chord position.   F power chord position.

Early Heavy Metal Rhythm Guitar

The following exercises are progressions that utilize this approach. Note that the chords are not sustained for very long, and that we are occasionally punctuating our rhythm work with some heavy single-note lines that are, in fact, often "doubles" of what the bassist is playing. This "doubling" effect was first popularized in three-man "power trios" during the late 1960s and early 1970s and is now a very common technique in heavy metal. If used properly, it can be extremely helpful in accentuating a band's "tightness."

80

Early Heavy Metal Rhythm Guitar

The two-note power chord approach has found its way into many classic guitar parts such as Dave Davies' "You Really Got Me" and "All Day and All of the Night," "Mississippi Queen" by Leslie West of Mountain, and numerous others.

Below are these three rhythm licks, played strictly in two-note power chord fashion. Both are in the styles of these two heavy metal founding fathers.

MORE ADVANCED POWER CHORD POSITIONS

Of course, not all chord forms within heavy metal are confined to two notes. Many guitarists, such as Pete Townshend of The Who and Jimmy Page of Led Zeppelin, helped popularize larger partial chord forms that were not only

Early Heavy Metal Rhythm Guitar

less harsh in nature than the two-note power chord approach, but also contained the third of the chord most of the time. The most popular of all these positions is based upon the open A chord form. Instead of the usual three fingers bunched up next to each other, the index finger covers the D, G, and B strings at the second fret in a partial barre form. This enables us to layer several other chord forms and notes over it, particularly the popular two-fingered C chord form (in this case of D). When the D chord is sounded, only the barred note (A) on the G string is left to ring. Here is an illustration of the partial barre chord form of A, with the D chord laid over it. Note the angle of the fingers.

D chord over A. Note index-finger barre for A chord.

PETE TOWNSHEND'S RIGHT-HAND FLOURISHES

While with The Who, Pete Townshend developed a very distinctive rhythm guitar style that was unique in its sound and its ability to create a great deal of dramatic musical tension. He would intersperse violent right-hand flourishes of power chords, while often maintaining constant open-string bass notes. You can hear these techniques in such Who classics as "Pinball Wizard," "I Can See for Miles," and "We Won't Get Fooled Again." The phrase often begins with the flourish, a series of rapid down-up-down strokes, followed by a sustained chord over eighth-note-droning constant bass notes. Below are a few examples of this technique. At first it'll be a bit difficult because the hand must be quite loose for the flourish, then you must abruptly shift positions and play the more rigid constant bass parts. When played properly this is one of those techniques that really enables you to sound like two guitarists at once!

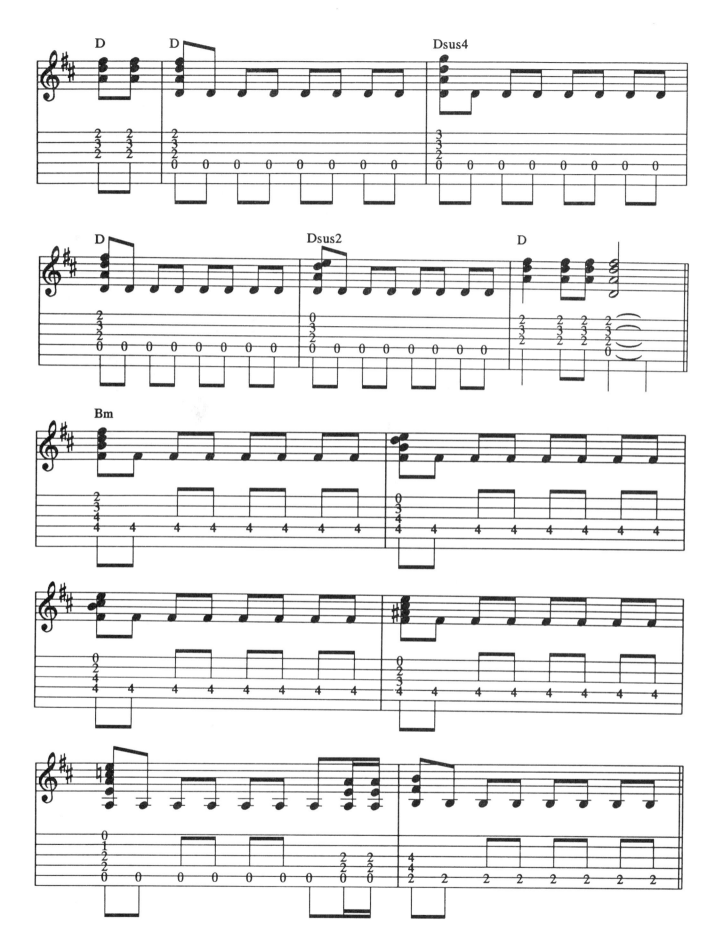

Early Heavy Metal Rhythm Guitar

Pete Townshend of The Who.
© Ebet Roberts, 1982.

THE CONSTANT BASS TECHNIQUE

The constant bass technique can be applied over the chords while moving up and down the neck. The open bass note allows us great freedom and mobility, as does the well-contained partial chord positions we are using. In this exercise, we see how the constant bass can be sustained over many new chord positions. The trick is to be able to strike the chords, and then return to the bass notes without losing a beat. Good luck!

▲ 85

Early Heavy Metal Rhythm Guitar

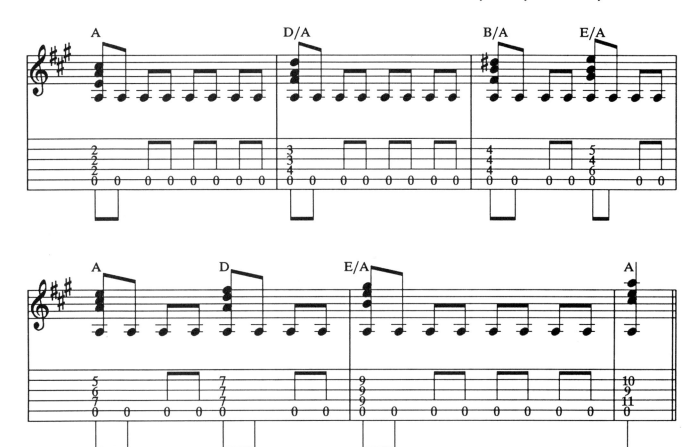

Early Heavy Metal Lead Guitar

Using the same scales I've given you, early heavy metal lead players drew heavily from the blues for both technical and musical ideas. Early influentials such as Jimmy Page, Jimi Hendrix, Jeff Beck, Leslie West, and Eric Clapton all possessed strong blues-based styles that, although they had the same roots, were as different as night and day. This was when the heavy metal sound took shape, and these important bands went through tremendous amounts of experimentation.

Many of the early metal lead guitarists were involved in a high-powered version of blues, and the licks and solos they formulated rarely stepped outside this range. Additional volume and sustain enabled these heavy metal pioneers to take string bending to new extremes, with tremendous emotional stretches and vibrato. Below are some of early heavy metal's most popular bend positions and licks. Note how so many of them require you first to commit the entire hand to the bend, and then suddenly play a flurry of normally fretted notes. This ability to quickly "get in and get out" of a bending situation is essential to great lead guitar playing.

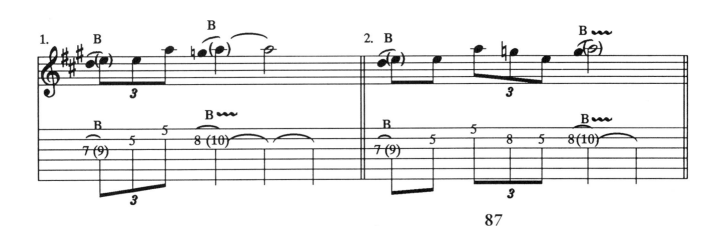

Early Heavy Metal Lead Guitar

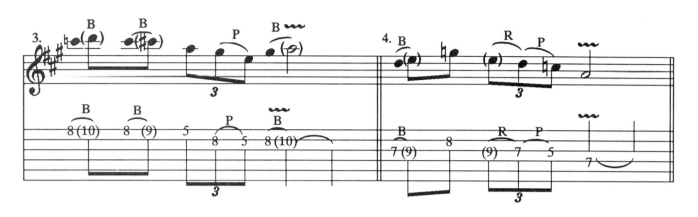

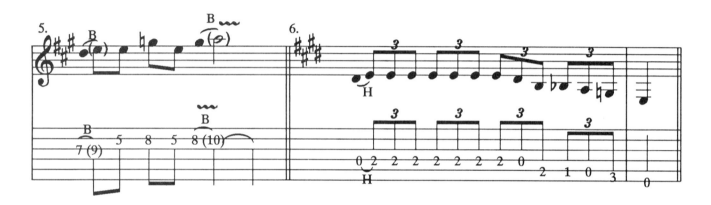

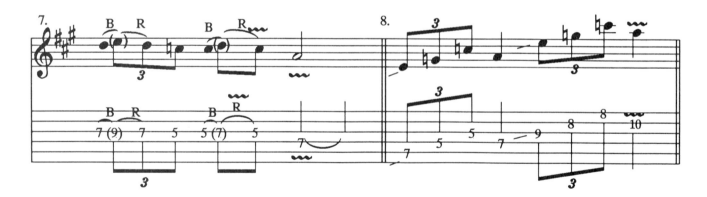

"OVERBENDING"

The term **overbending** simply refers to bends that go beyond the normal note you are bending to. These are bends of pure emotion, but you must remember that they are musical as well, and have specific notes that they "overbend" to. Your hands must be strengthened from a lot of bending to tackle these without tearing up your skin. And again, I must emphasize the importance of *proper* bending technique when executing these overbends. Take note of precisely which note you're bending to, and exactly what position you're bending from. One thing in your favor is that it will be pretty hard to overshoot your mark. You also now have the ability to train your ear, and listen to exactly what note you are reaching with the bend. Since these bends are much less frequently used than the traditional half and whole-step bends, your fingers probably will not develop a feel for exactly how far to bend them ahead of time. This is where your ear development comes into play, as you must rely on it to tell you just how far is far enough!

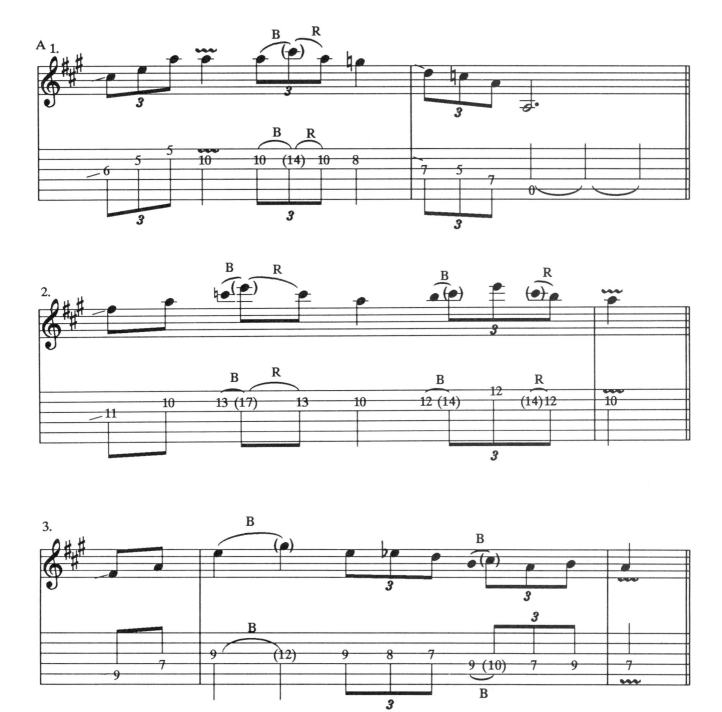

Early Heavy Metal Lead Guitar

"Overbending" the G string. Note the thumb's position as it applies opposite pressure.

EARLY HEAVY METAL "FLASH"

Many aspects of the licks we're about to play are still so prevalent in heavy metal lead guitar that it's really a misnomer to call them *early*. They were developed in the mid to late 1960s by such players as Jeff Beck, Eric Clapton, and Jimmy Page and to this day, act as strong foundations for some of metal's finest exponents.

Most of these licks are based upon a simple yet effective use of partial barres with rapid hammer-ons and pull-offs placed over them. Once you hear them you'll recognize them as old friends immediately! They are also great stretch exercises for the left hand. Please attempt to execute these as third-finger stretches, but should this prove a bit too difficult for you (especially on the wider frets) by all means use the pinky. I advocate the third finger simply because it's stronger and is more apropos of a blues-based technique such as this. Remember only to barre over as many strings as needed with your first finger. Good luck!

Early Heavy Metal Lead Guitar

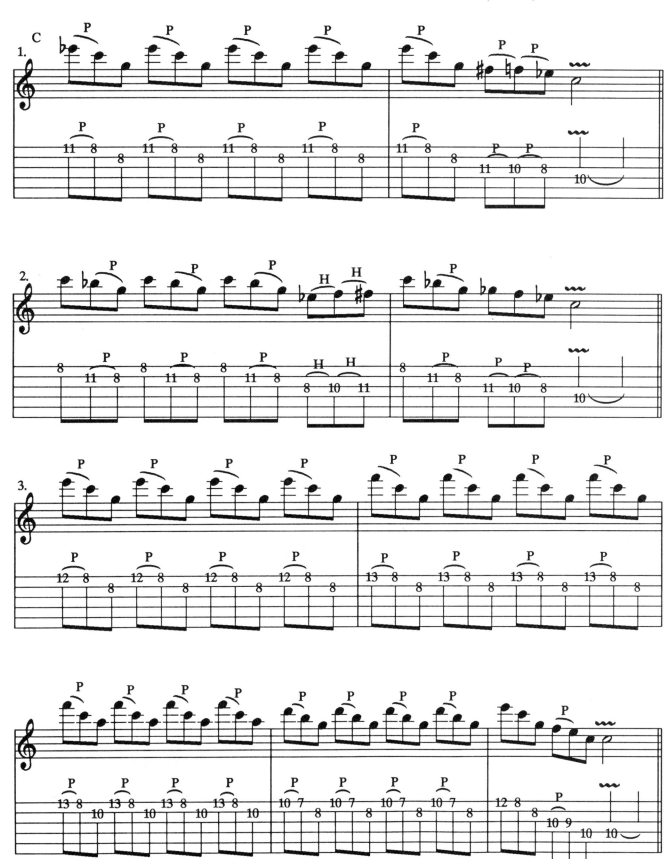

Early Heavy Metal Lead Guitar

Jeff Beck, one of rock guitar's true innovators.
© Ebet Roberts, 1983.

YOUR FIRST HEAVY METAL LEAD SOLOS

Now is a good time for you to begin putting everything we've covered into perspective with some soloing. As opposed to the blues solos we tackled earlier, these are based on more heavy metal-like progressions, and utilize the aggressive approach usually associated with heavy metal lead guitar. You'll notice quite a lot of the "flash" licks and positions being used, as well as many of the bends and "overbends" we discussed. I hope you have fun with them, but please don't try to tackle too much too soon. If you feel that you might need some extra work in a certain department, please feel free to go back to the applicable section and do so. Remember, the things I'm teaching you in this book took years to develop for me and the other guitarists mentioned, so don't expect to get it all overnight!

▲ 93

Early Heavy Metal Lead Guitar

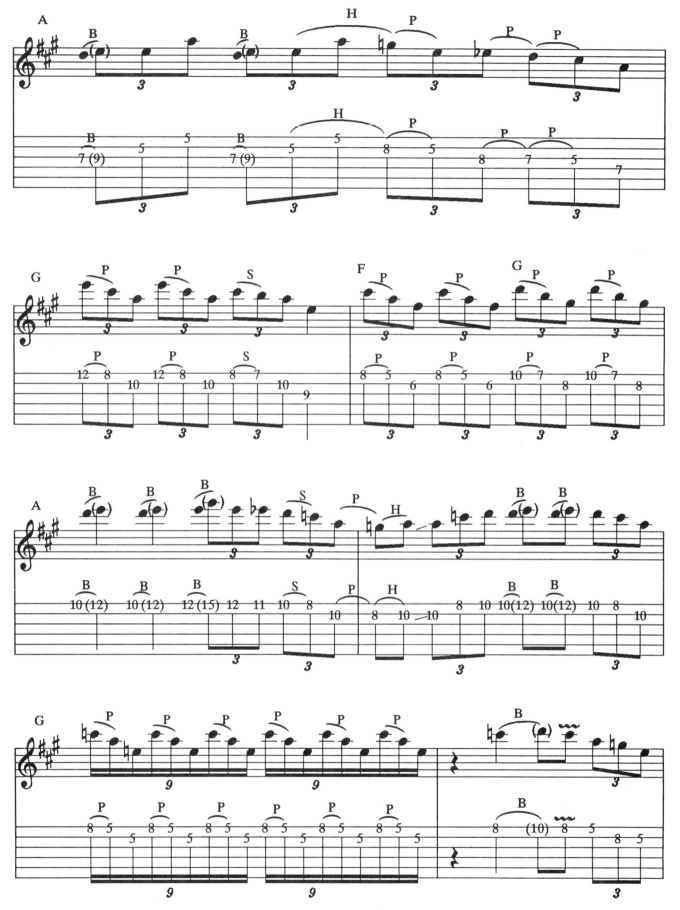

Early Heavy Metal Lead Guitar

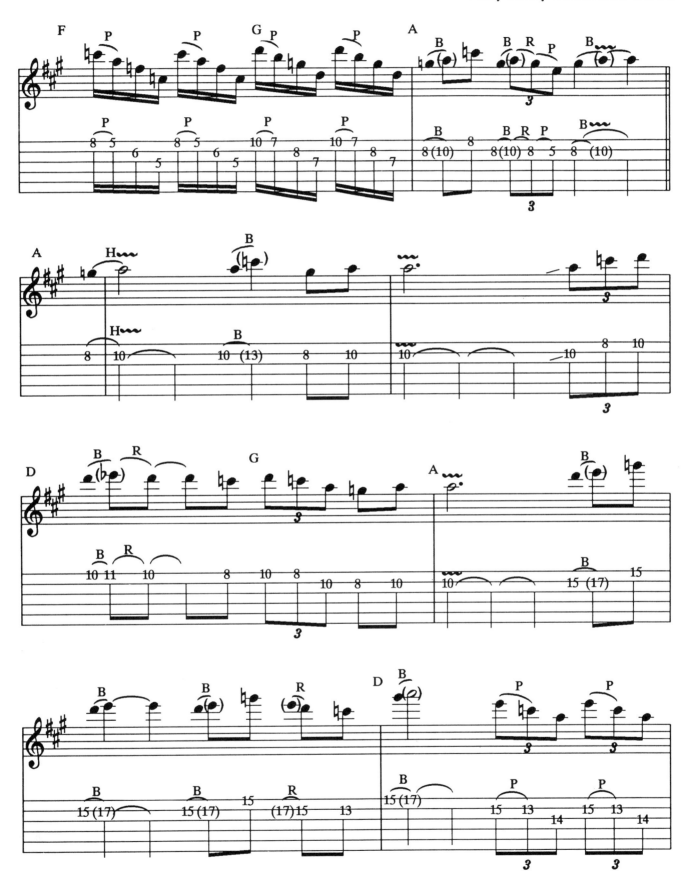

Early Heavy Metal Lead Guitar

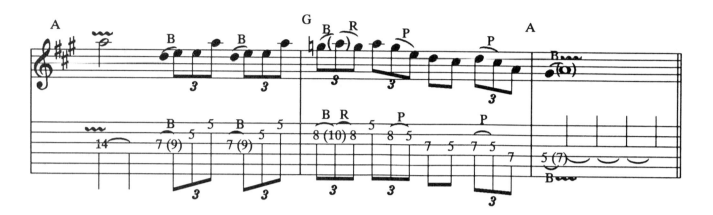

ROCK'S FIRST "GUITAR GODS"

I think it is important to study the true impact that the playing of some of heavy metal's early greats has had. These players' influence on contemporary guitarists remains as strong as ever and Jimmy Page and Eric Clapton continue to make musical contributions today. Needless to say, they are literally deified by thousands of guitarists the world over!

JIMMY PAGE

Jimmy Page, who first gained widespread recognition with Led Zeppelin, is perhaps the first guitarist to *define* the heavy metal sound. His power-chord rhythm guitar work and incredibly flashy and fast (for the time) lead work on songs such as "Rock Me" and "Stairway to Heaven" helped inspire an entire generation of aspiring guitar heroes. I'm happy to say that at the time of this writing he's embarked on a solo career and with a brand new album has once again burst upon the scene. I strongly suggest that you listen to any material recorded by Page to gain a greater appreciation of one of heavy metal's major pioneers.

Jimmy Page of Led Zeppelin and the Firm, playing his legendary Gibson double-neck.
© Ebet Roberts, 1983.

97

Jimmy Page's guitars have always been of the traditional nature, and he caused the sunburst Les Paul to become the first electric guitar heavily associated with heavy metal playing. He also uses early Telecasters and Danelectro guitars, and even popularized the "double-neck" guitar by using one on "Stairway to Heaven." This guitar, a Gibson SG style, consists of a standard six-string neck as well as a twelve-string neck.

In the exercises that follow, I've set down a series of licks in the style of Jimmy Page with some of his most recognizable trademark sounds. You'll hear how strongly their influence can be heard in today's playing.

JIMI HENDRIX

Without a doubt, Jimi Hendrix is the most revered guitarist ever. This is due in part to the fact that his life was lost at such an early age, cutting short this creative genius' incredible contribution, but mostly it's due to the amazing legacy of work he left. No guitarist has ever combined so much raw emotion with such innovativeness and "flash" as Hendrix did, and his playing was a testament to the electric guitar's awesome capabilities. He still influences thousands of new players in the 1990s. Stars such as Eddie Van Halen, Steve Vai, Joe Satriani, the late Stevie Ray Vaughan, and countless others also owe so much to his innovations of some twenty years ago.

Jimi Hendrix.
© Tom Copi.

It must be said that his versatility was unequaled. This becomes apparent as you go from his soulful rhythm and blues style on "The Wind Cries Mary," to his awesome blues approach on Dylan's "All Along the Watchtower," to the screaming, wrenching, unearthly tones on "Star-Spangled Banner." Whatever Jimi needed to get out of his guitar, he got—whether it was getting feedback, shaking the whammy bar wildly, or even pouring lighter fluid on it and setting it ablaze! This last example was a theatrical move that usually ended his shows and, coupled with wildly screaming feedback, often left audiences awestruck! If you ever get the chance to see the late 1960s film "Monterey Pop," do so—you'll see one of Jimi's most extraordinary performances while in his prime.

The following group of runs illustrates some of the more trademark Hendrix guitar parts. Pick up his classic recordings such as "The Wind Cries Mary," "All Along the Watchtower," "Foxy Lady," and "Fire" to hear his particular treatment. There are simply so many aspects to the Hendrix sound that cannot be conveyed on the printed page; you must hear them to get their full impact!

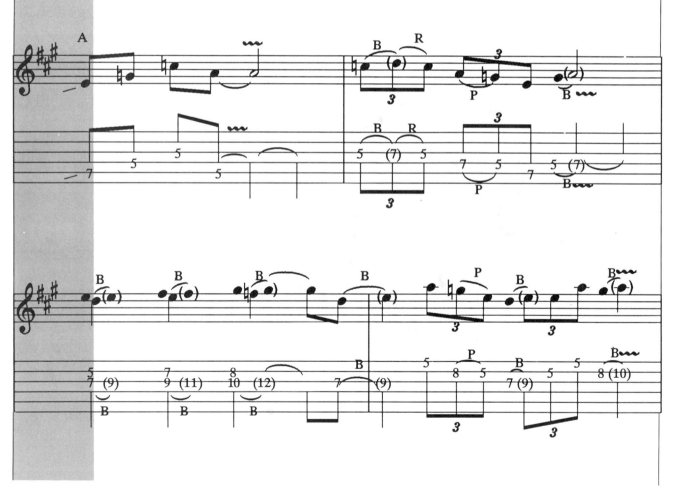

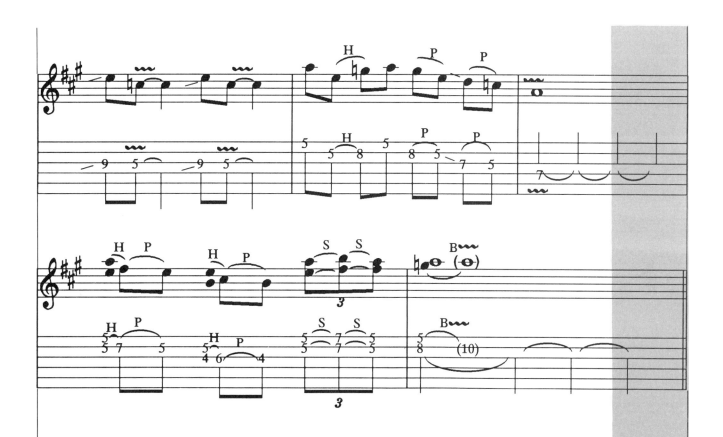

ERIC CLAPTON

As lead guitarist with John Mayall's Bluesbreakers and then the Yardbirds, Eric Clapton started to forge a sterling reputation as one of the England's, and the world's finest guitarists. However, it was with his breakthrough power trio, Cream (with Jack Bruce and Ginger Baker), that Clapton gained worldwide acclaim as one of rock guitar's true innovators. Clapton's style has always remained closer to it's roots than that of his peers Jimmy Page and Jeff Beck, and the influence of B.B. King, Buddy Guy, and Otis Rush can clearly be heard in his work to this day.

With the band Cream, he and Jack Bruce helped pave the way for the importance of lead guitar and bass "doubling" in rock and heavy metal music. This is most apparent in their classic hit, "Sunshine of Your Love." Always an evolving player, Clapton had many other projects, including Blind Faith and Derek and the Dominos, which yielded perhaps his greatest classic, "Layla" (a song that also featured the important slide guitar work of Duane Allman).

Clapton is still as important a player as ever, and he continues to forge new territory for himself. However, there is no denying that his early work, especially with Cream, made him perhaps the foremost hero to many of today's heavy metal greats.

The following is a group of distinctive Eric Clapton guitar phrases. Note the use of heavy left-hand vibrato. This should be used in the downward "pivoting" motion I discussed earlier.

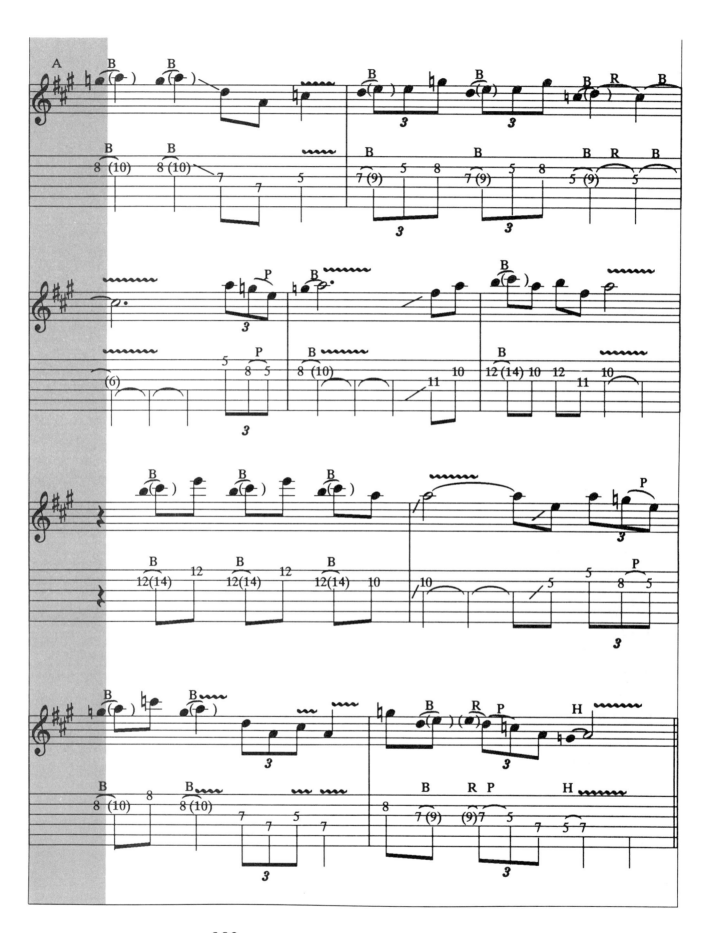

SEVEN

Contemporary Heavy Metal Guitar

With the advent of players like Eddie Van Halen, Steve Vai, Vinnie Moore, Yngwie Malmsteen, and others, the notion of "heavy metal lead guitarist" has taken on several new dimensions. The use of classically oriented scales and hand positions, as well as other modern "flash" techniques such as right-hand tapping, harmonics, whammy bar tricks, and extremely fast picking are all making heavy metal lead guitar a very new frontier.

Vinnie Moore, one of heavy metal guitar's brightest new talents.

It is true that there exists a sameness in much of what is recorded these days and labeled "heavy metal," but the fault lies more with the record companies and producers than the guitar-slingers and bands. The problem is that for the first time this musical form has become a really big seller. In the record industry, this immediately creates a cloning situation in which "formulas" are devised for making the "perfect" metal record (or so they think). This situation has disenchanted many true heavy metal followers who have dismissed many of the new successful "metal" bands as merely pop groups in a heavy metal guise. This cloning situation has also trickled down to the guitarists themselves to the point that one almost expects to hear a certain combination of techniques and tricks in a lead guitar solo! Music videos have contributed to this shortage of variety, in that one expects a certain degree of visual sameness to these solos as well. On the bright side, at least, this cloning approach has created a style for players to "shoot for" when developing their heavy metal soloing skills and stage prowess. I know that someday one of you will change all of this "sameness" in heavy metal guitar by putting your own special "brand" on it.

THE VARIOUS SCALE MODES

One of the most useful ways of gaining an understanding of the origins of many scales is to see how they relate to the *diatonic* major scale. By doing this, we can see the scale modes as different positions of the original scale, only placed against different chords. The names—Ionian, Dorian, Phrygian, Lydian, Mixolydian, Aeolian, and Locrian—may appear a bit mysterious at first, but once we can play and experiment with them, the mysteries will unfold for you.

These seven names represent the seven ways in which the major scale can be played. Each time we play one we are simply shifting the importance of the notes by beginning and ending on different notes that are within the scale itself. Juxtapose these against the chords that share the name with the modal scale's first note, and we can get some dramatic effects.

First, let's get acquainted with the all-important major scale, in this case for the key of C. In the modal framework, we'll refer to this as the **Ionian** scale. Here are several positions, both open and closed, for this major scale.

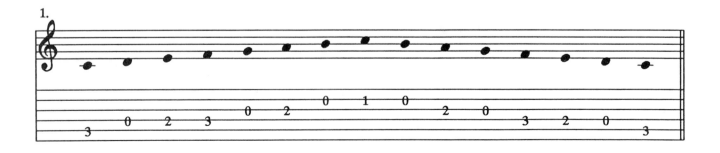

Contemporary Heavy Metal Guitar

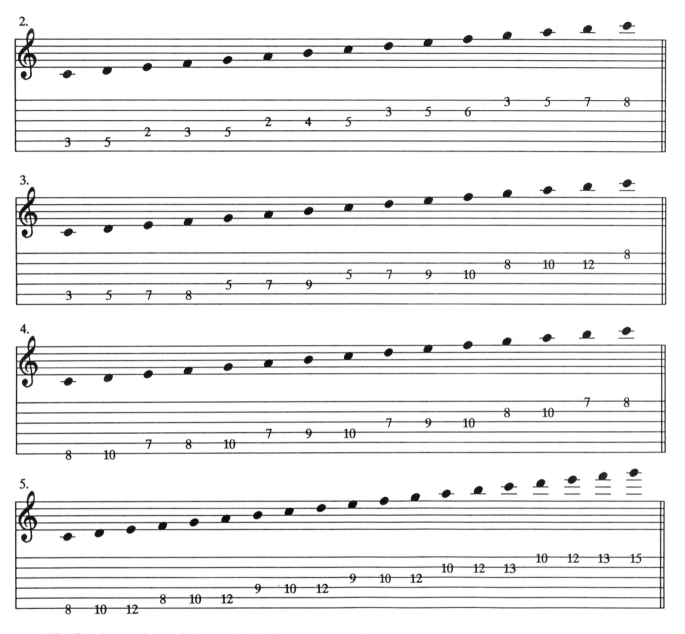

The **Dorian** scale mode has a decidedly *minor* sound to it when played against the Dm chord. This scale always begins with the second note of the original major Ionian scale.

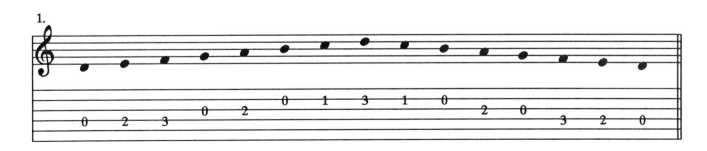

Contemporary Heavy Metal Guitar

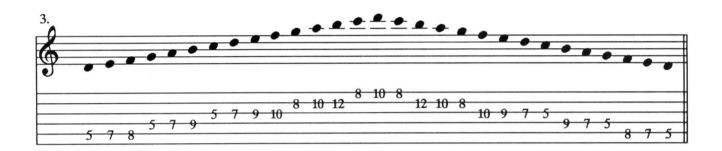

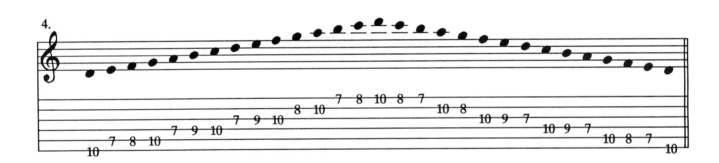

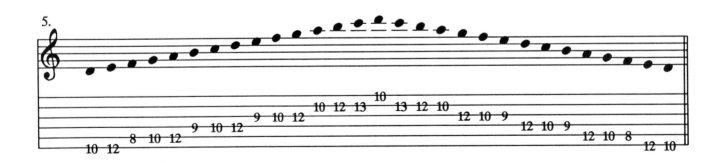

The **Phrygian** mode is also minor in nature when applied to Em, and the half-step E to F within the scale lends an eerie, dissonant effect.

▲ 107

Contemporary Heavy Metal Guitar

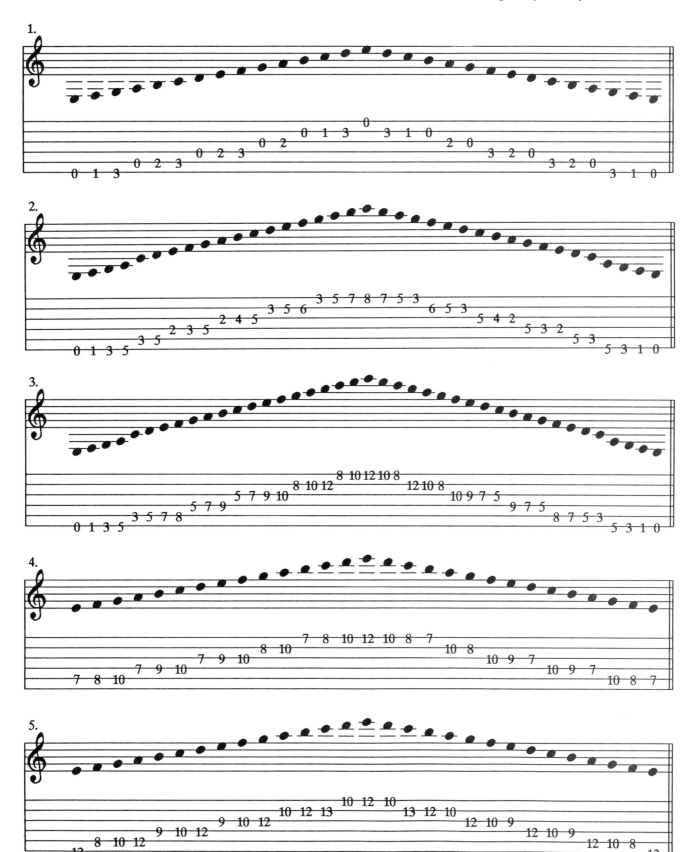

Contemporary Heavy Metal Guitar

The **Lydian** scale, which begins on an F, relates quite strongly to an F major seventh chord due to the presence of an E note. This scale is still the original C scale, only now the notes are moved up a full *fourth*.

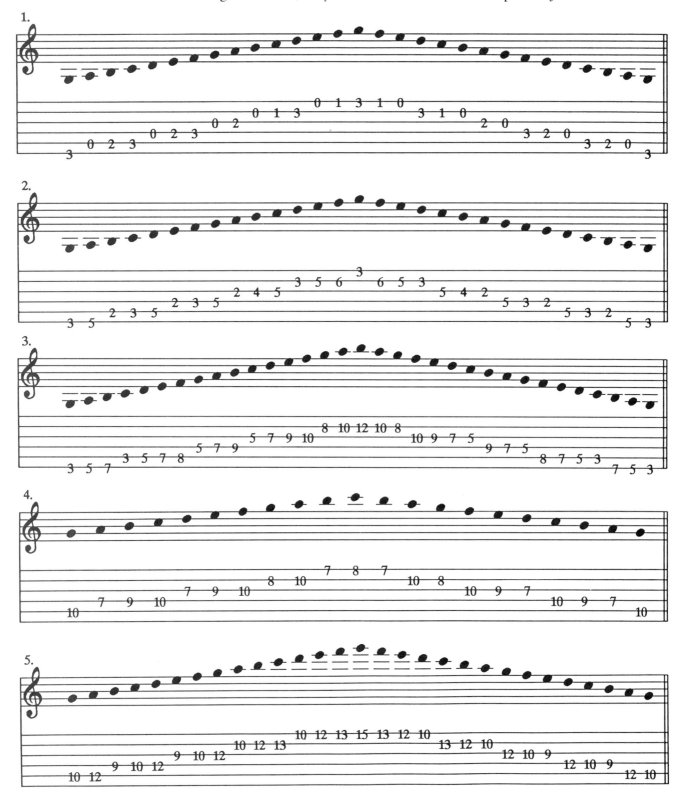

Just as the Lydian scale was up a fourth from the Ionian, the **Mixolydian** scale, starting on G, is up a *fifth*. Placed over a G chord, this scale's combination of an F natural (flatted seventh) and B (major third) creates some unique improvisational ideas.

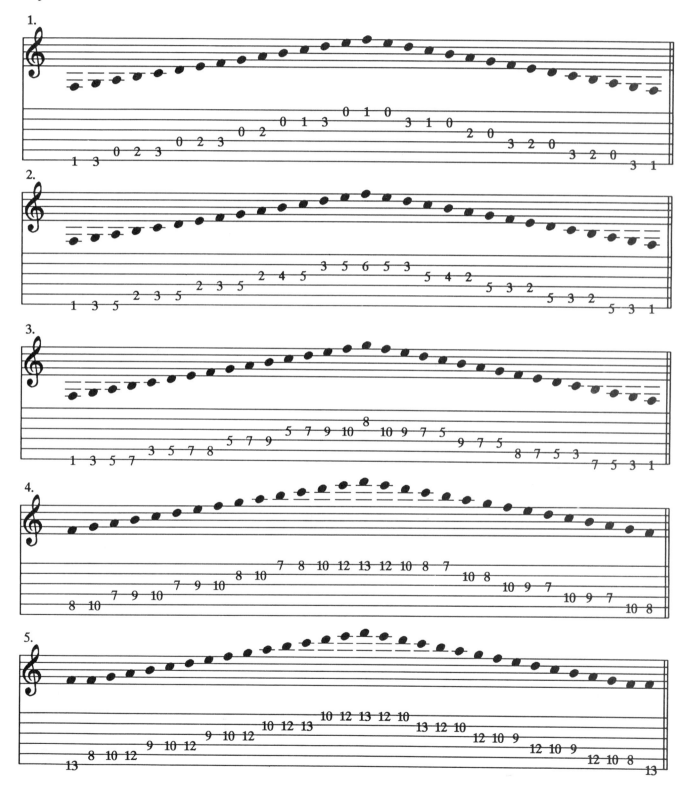

Contemporary Heavy Metal Guitar

The **Aeolian** scale also has a minor feeling, with the F natural adding another unusual note to the picture. Be sure to play an Am chord just before practicing this scale so you can hear its effect.

1.
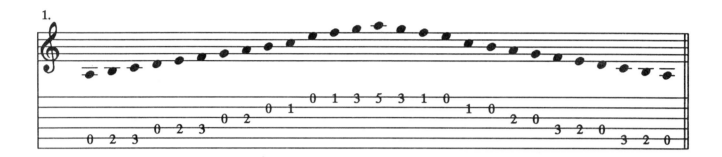

2.

3.
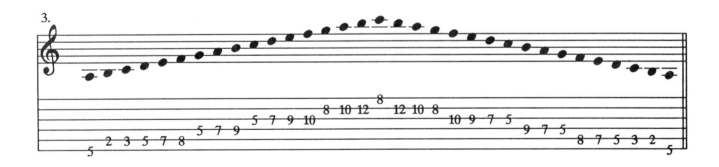

4.
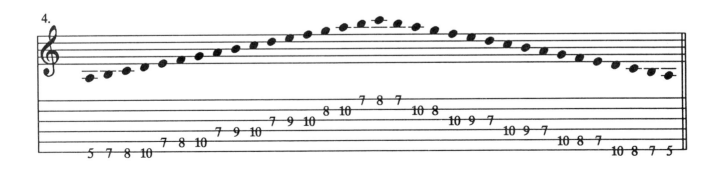

▲ 111

Contemporary Heavy Metal Guitar

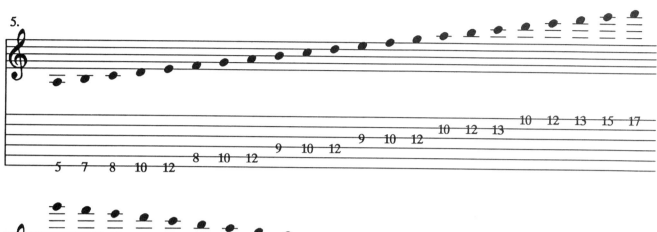

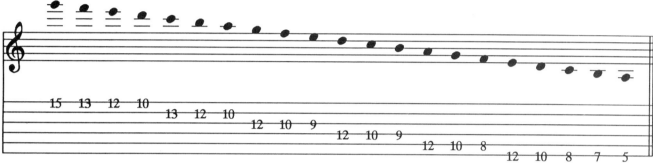

Containing the half-steps between B and C as well as E and F, the B **Locrian** mode has perhaps the most unusual sound of all. It will probably remind you of some of the scales used in Middle and Far Eastern music.

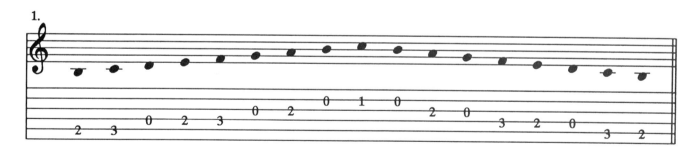

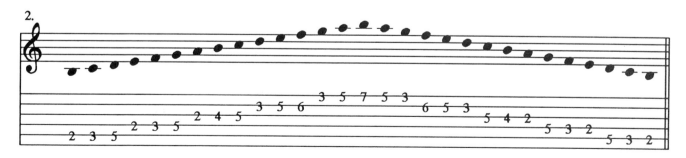

Contemporary Heavy Metal Guitar

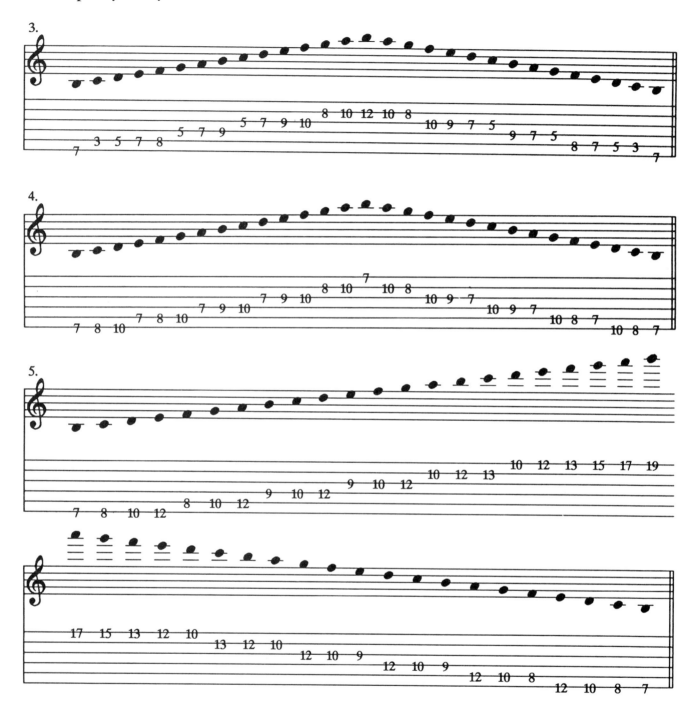

IMPROVISING USING THE MODES

The mode approach towards soloing and improvisation has been brought to the forefront of heavy metal by such players as Steve Vai, Yngwie Malmsteen, and newcomers Tony McAlpine and Vinnie Moore. It has proven to be a very refreshing change of pace from the standard pentatonic scales, and has opened doors for lead guitar and rock itself.

Contemporary Heavy Metal Guitar

You'll find that once you've gotten used to where the scales lie beneath your fingers, this improvisational tool will begin to take on true meaning. This will most notably occur when you can recognize the notes and their relationship to the root. This is known as **relative pitch,** and it's something that can only come with years of experience. Of course, once you know what the given note should sound like, you should know by instinct where it lies within the scale position you've chosen. This is where modal exercises pay off, for you learn to truly recognize the various notes and their changes in value depending on which chord you are playing against.

First let's try a heavy metal solo in D minor, using the Dorian mode. Note how I've consciously designed the exercise to shift positions around the neck, while maintaining the Dorian approach.

Contemporary Heavy Metal Guitar

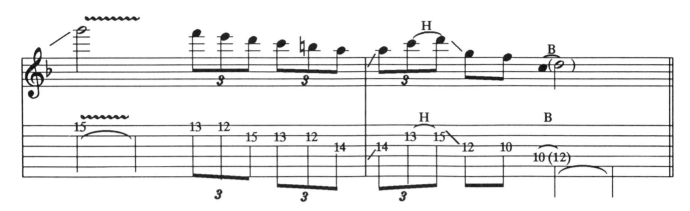

Next, is a solo in the Phrygian mode, with a strong emphasis on the scale position that lies in the middle of the neck. Note that we are still using a lot of hammer-ons and pull-offs even though now the emphasis is on picking each note in rapid succession.

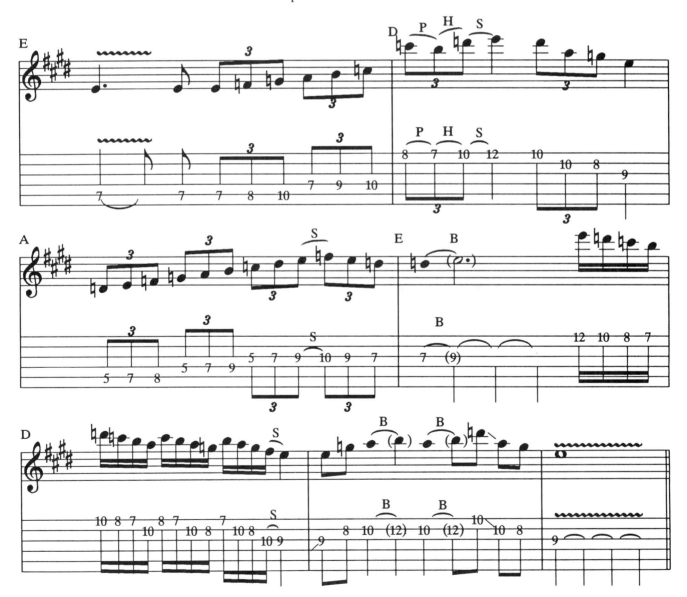

Contemporary Heavy Metal Guitar

The Lydian mode is very major sounding, and in this rather aggressive exercise we see how closely in feeling it relates to the original major scale. Remember to keep the picking hand relaxed in order to facilitate the quickness required for this kind of playing.

Contemporary Heavy Metal Guitar

This exercise uses the G Mixolydian mode for a very bluesy effect, with its flatted seventh combined with a major third.

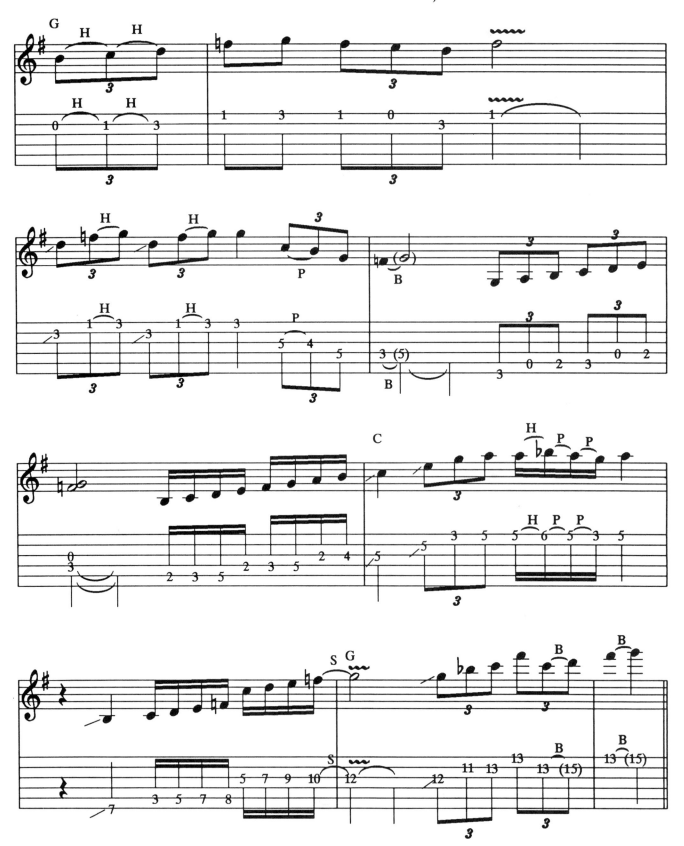

Using the A Aeolian mode we create a very minor feeling. This mournful emotion is further enhanced by the F natural in this scale.

This solo features the Middle Eastern-sounding Locrian mode. This mode is very popular with players such as Steve Vai and Yngwie Malmsteen, and this solo is inspired by their particular brand of playing.

Contemporary Heavy Metal Guitar

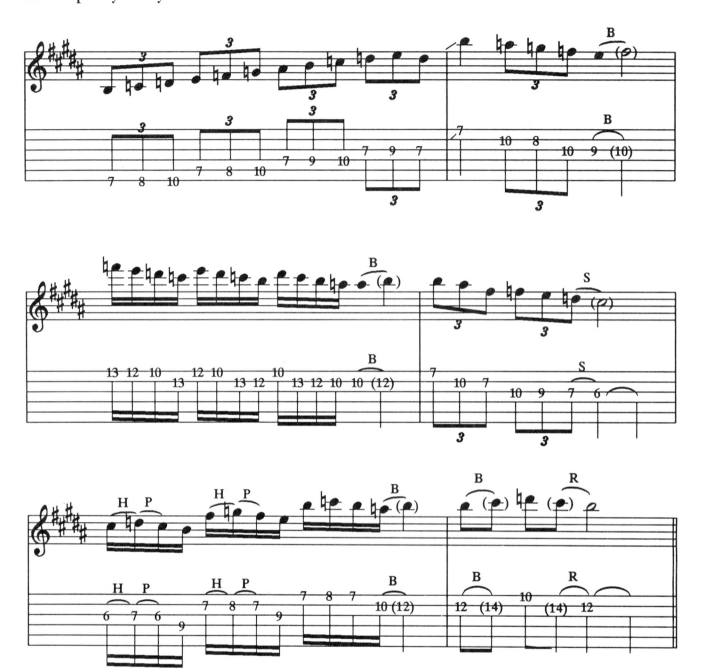

THE HARMONIC MINOR SCALE

No discussion of contemporary guitar styles would be complete without mentioning the harmonic minor scale. This is one of the more challenging scales to work with, and offers much in the way of melodic possibilities. There are five basic fingering patterns to learn for the harmonic minor scale. They are below for the key of C, both ascending and descending the fingerboard. No-

Yngwie Malmsteen.
© Ebet Roberts, 1985.

tice that the main notes we emphasize are the minor third, the flatted sixth, and the major seventh. Together these notes create the unusual tonality unique to the harmonic minor scale. In fact, the one and a half-step jump between the flatted sixth and the sharp seventh is a unique (and difficult to remember) facet of the scale. Because of these extreme jumps, it's necessary to get your hand used to the many *stretches* it must perform. Therefore, the "s" used in these exercises will stand for a "stretch" of the hand for positioning, rather than its previous usage for "slides" between notes.

120

Contemporary Heavy Metal Guitar

1.

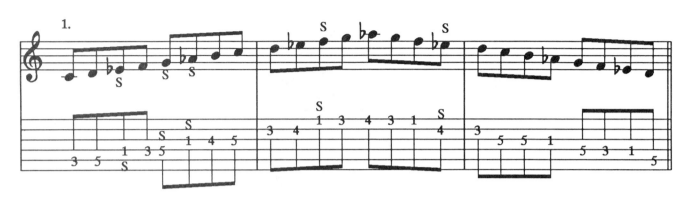

2.

3.

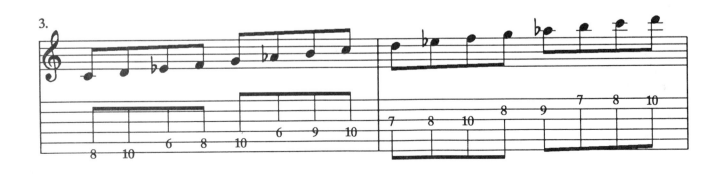

Contemporary Heavy Metal Guitar

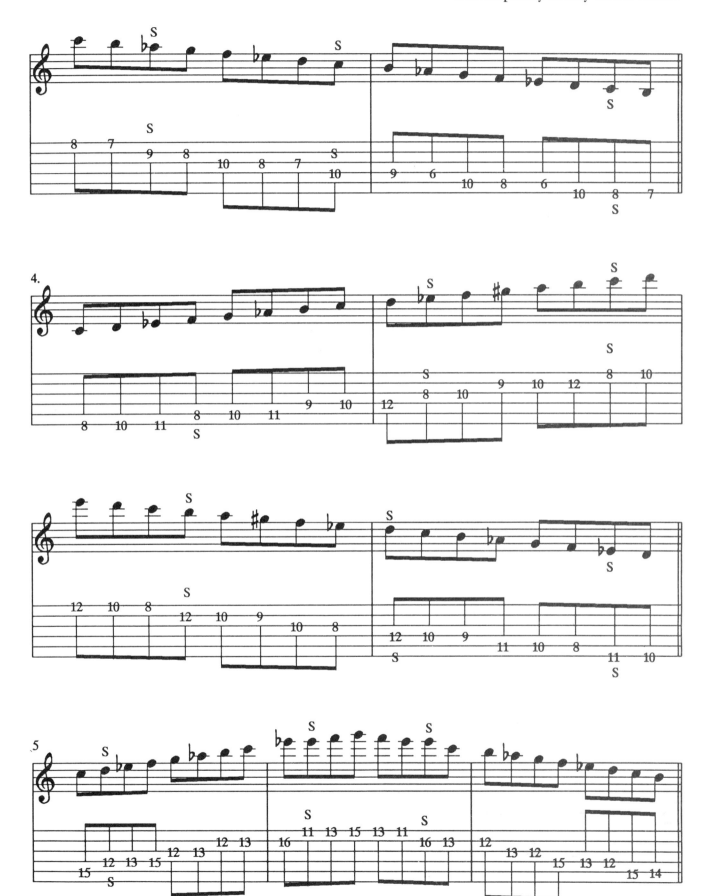

Contemporary Heavy Metal Guitar

Next we have a solo based on the harmonic minor scales we just learned. Beware of the many built-in stretches, signified by an "s," that will truly test the limits of your left hand!

THE VIBRATO OR "WHAMMY" BAR

Few guitar gadgets have enjoyed as much of a roller-coaster type of popularity as the vibrato arm. These days it has many bizarre nicknames such as "whammy bar," "wang bar," and "dip stick." This tremolo (or vibrato unit) was first used during the early and mid-1950s by players such as Merle Travis and Chet Atkins to produce Hawaiian-like sounds on the guitar. It regained popularity in the 1960s when it was employed by surf–sounding groups such as The Ventures, The Surfaris, and the king of twang himself, Duane Eddy.

The vibrato bar is a device which is a part of the bridge assembly of many guitars that enables you to produce a wavering, vibrato-like effect by releasing the tension of the strings and returning them to their original pitch. The first solid-body guitar to come with this as standard equipment was the Fender Stratocaster in 1954. However, it wasn't until the "surf" sound came into vogue in the 1960s that this device became truly popular both as a novelty and as a serious additional sound in the guitar's repertoire.

One of the vibrato arm's major problems has always been that it tends to knock the strings out of tune. This can make live performances unbearable due to the time spent constantly retuning strings. In today's heavy metal playing, the whammy bar serves an even more important role as a "flash" device. It's increasing significance meant something had to be done about the tuning situation. Something *was* done, thanks to people like Floyd Rose and Kahler, who invented a "locking" tremolo arm that does not put the strings out of tune, no matter how extreme one uses it. With this unit, the strings behind the nut are secured into a fixed tension so there can be no slippage from the constant loosening and tightening of the strings. As a result, the tuning of the strings now takes place down on the bridge itself, as the tuners on the headstock are rendered useless by the locking nut. Installing one of these locking units requires a lot of changes made to the guitar itself, so you're best off getting a guitar with one already on it, or at least installing it on a newer, not too valuable guitar. Being a vintage guitar collector myself, this is not a modification I would recommend doing to a stock, vintage instrument!

Here is a photo of a vintage Fender Stratocaster with one of the first production tremolo bars.

Early tremolo unit on a 1957 Strat.

The ideal position for playing with a whammy bar is to be picking with the right hand while actually touching the arm itself with your other fingers. It's crucial that the bar have a loose feel here, for we don't want to inhibit the right hand's ability to reach all of the strings with a fluid motion. This technique keeps the vibrato arm ready at all times for either subtle single-note work or the more extreme metal techniques being used today thanks to the brilliant pioneering on the part of Jimi Hendrix. Note the subtle way in which my right hand is both picking the string and holding the vibrato bar in "ready" position.

Position for holding the vibrato bar while using the flatpick.

WHAMMY BAR EXERCISES

Since the pitch we are creating is mostly cause for conjecture, it will be difficult to write out the actual notes in the music and tab. Rather, you should rely upon my description of the given approach, be it subtle wavering vibrato, screaming "dive-bombs," or whatever the case may be.

As a "getting acquainted" exercise with the vibrato bar, you should just try to play an open A chord, while maintaining a great deal of control over the bar. Try to create a nice, even vibrato where the pitch changes are consistent with the actual rhythmic pulse of the bar's movement.

In the next exercise, I want you to use the same position, but strike the chord harder, and make each beat of the vibrato arm a more extreme "dip" with a more frenzied, aggressive sound. This is a technique very reminiscent of Jimi Hendrix's approach.

In this example play a chord arpeggiated (one note at a time), introducing the vibrato effect to each note as it's played. This will be an aid in developing your touch for picking the strings while holding the bar in your hand.

Here we see how single-note licks can be accentuated by well-placed vibrato arm technique. It is still best to play these with the arm in "ready" position, so you're not futilely grabbing for the arm when you need it. In the case of these licks, only a subtle use of the arm is required—just dipping the strings ever so slightly for the desired effect.

Contemporary Heavy Metal Guitar

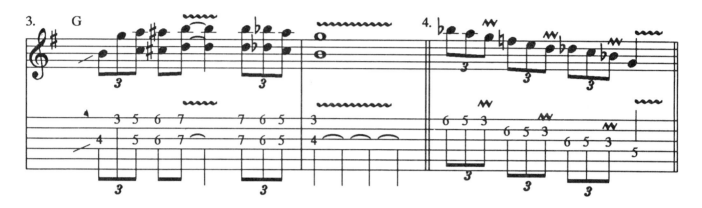

Power chords can be strongly accentuated with roaring vibrato arm technique. This is a very common style used in todays' heavy metal by both lead and rhythm players alike. Below are a few examples of this style. This will require aggressive dips with the arm, but with a quick delivery and only slight slackening of the strings.

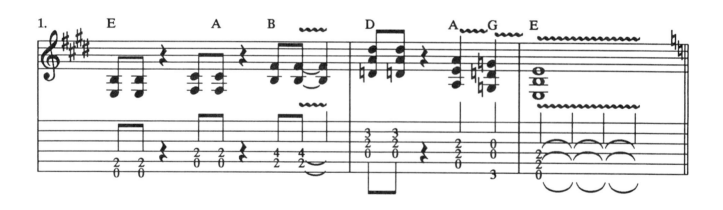

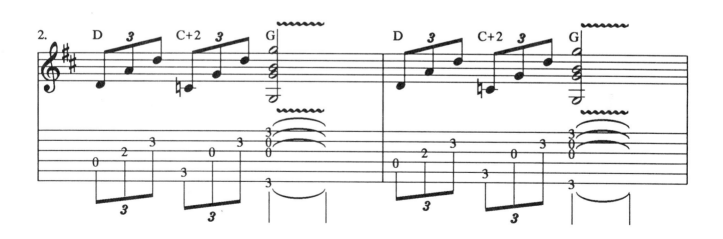

Contemporary Heavy Metal Guitar

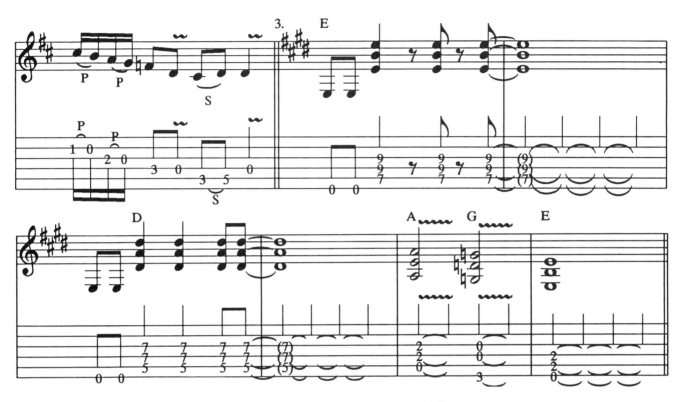

The solo below is in the style of such heavy metal greats as Eddie Van Halen and Steve Vai and illustrates how one can use the whammy bar to punctuate specific moments within a solo context. Keep in mind that this is usually played at very high volumes, often causing **feedback** (continual send-and-return of sound between a guitar pickup and amp that can become incredibly piercing if not controlled). The vibrato arm is frequently used during long, sustaining notes and the ability to "dip" the notes below pitch helps to contain the feedback and keep it from running away. If you're having trouble achieving this feedback effect, try turning the guitar towards the amp while sustaining a note with vibrato. When the feedback reaches powerful proportions, start to waver the note slowly with the vibrato arm, and take note of how that action controls the feedback. You may have to search around the guitar for the right note to feedback, as some will be more prone than others.

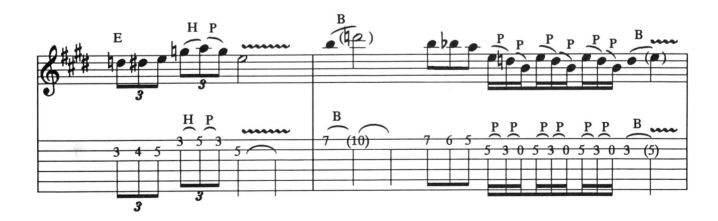

Contemporary Heavy Metal Guitar

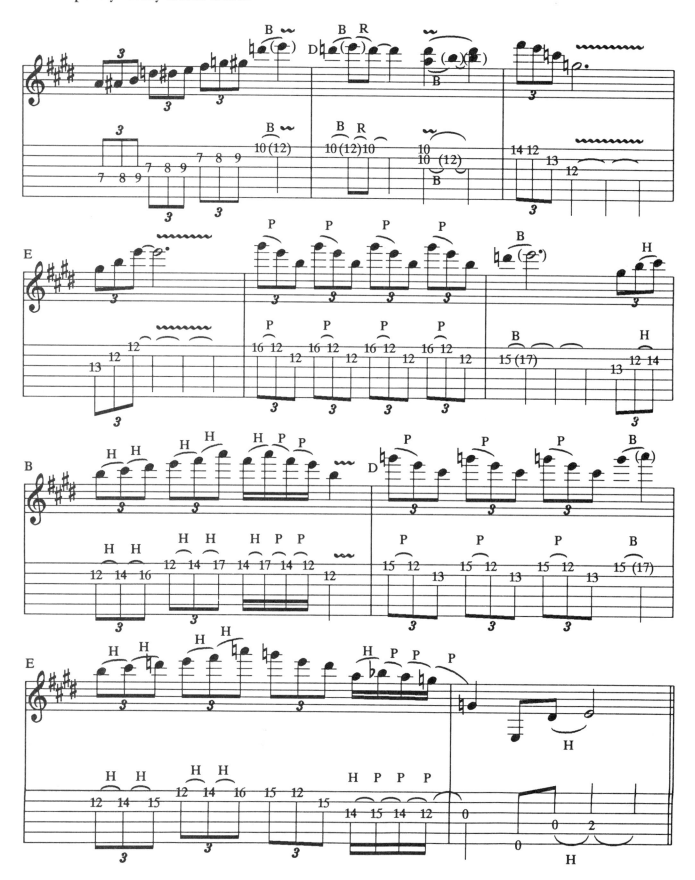

Contemporary Heavy Metal Guitar

USING HARMONICS IN HEAVY METAL GUITAR

The bell-like "chimes" that can be created on the guitar at various frets known as harmonics can be of great use in louder lead guitar styles such as heavy metal. They can take on an aggressive tone when attacked the right way, plus they can be very effective when used in conjunction with a vibrato bar.

Many guitarists, such as Steve Vai, Bruce Kulick of Kiss, and Brad Gillis, and Jeff Watson of Night Ranger, like to use screaming harmonics in their solos. The extremely loud volumes at which these performers play enable them to bring out certain harmonics and overtones that would not even be heard on a guitar played at lower volumes.

Warren DiMartini of the group Ratt, just after striking some harmonics.
© Ebet Roberts, 1985.

Let's take a look at how and where harmonics are created on the guitar. You must *lightly* touch the string directly over the metal fret itself and then release it *immediately* after the note is plucked. This will allow the string to ring true and not be damped in any way. The easiest harmonics to create are at the twelfth fret, creating a perfect second octave above the open strings and the *same* notes that would occur if we fretted at those frets.

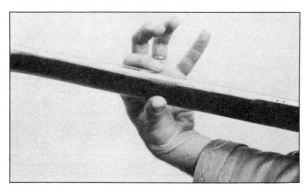

Touching a harmonic directly over the metal fret.

Contemporary Heavy Metal Guitar

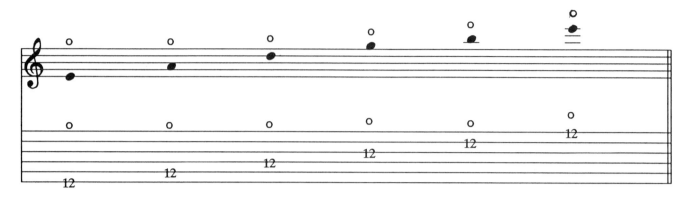

Harmonics can also be created quite easily at the seventh fret. These also duplicate the notes we can press down here, only this time they're an octave *higher* than the standard notes we can play.

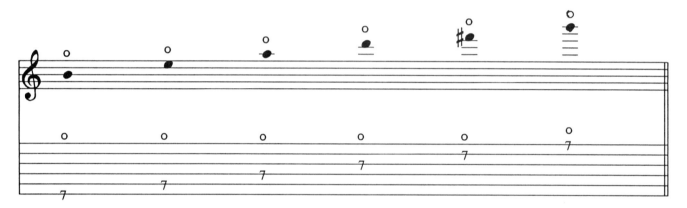

On the fifth fret, we have some harmonics that are even harder to get to ring properly, due to their high tonal range. This is also the only one of the "big three" harmonic locations that creates notes that are totally different than the *actual* notes that would occur should the strings be pressed down at that fret. In this case, we get an even *higher* octave than the one we created at the twelfth fret. It should also be noted that these can all be played an octave (or twelve frets) up from these positions. Therefore, the twenty-fourth, the nineteenth, and the seventeenth frets are just as usable for similar results.

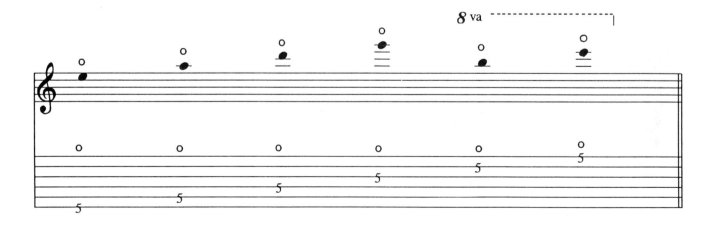

Obviously, the deeper the sound of the string, the easier it is to create clear harmonics. As an experiment, I would like you to play harmonics at each fret of the low E string, with the exception of the first fret, which will not give any harmonic at all. Some of these must be plucked very hard, and knowing when to lift your finger will be critical to your results. Then try to create harmonics at the same frets on all the other strings, while trying to identify their note values. You'll most likely find some unexpected surprises lurking around your guitar, as you'll be creating some harmonic notes that seemingly have *no* relationship to the fret you are playing over at the time! Experiment with these sounds, and be sure to try some of them with the vibrato bar as well—the combination can be sensational!

In the following exercise, we'll explore some of the uses of both harmonics and whammy bar techniques as employed by such artists as Brad Gillis and Jeff Watson of Night Ranger, Steve Vai, and Bruce Kulick of Kiss. The lower strings can produce a kind of "roaring" effect, while the higher ones can conjure up more scream-like tonalities. I would like you to experiment as much as possible with these, particularly in terms of how far you go with the whammy bar. You may want to play note with a subtle sustaining vibrato, while the next note becomes a harmonic "dive-bomb" (as my friend Bruce Kulick calls it) wherein the whammy bar is used to lower the sustaining note as if it's falling from space. This was one of the truly dynamic styles Jimi Hendrix created.

Bruce Kulick of Kiss playing a Strat-style ESP.

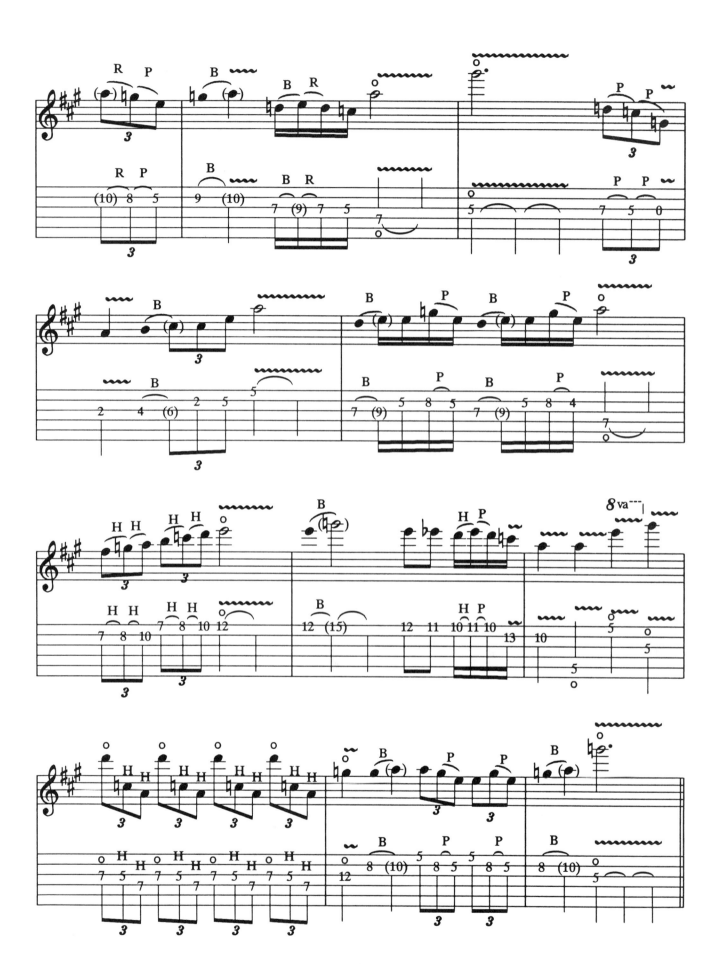

RIGHT-HAND TAPPING

Right-hand tapping, or the right-handed hammer-on, is without doubt the most celebrated and recognizable style within lead guitar playing today. Popularized and perfected by Eddie Van Halen and Randy Rhoads among others, right-hand tapping was actually used for years by jazz greats such as Tal Farlow without nearly the widespread recognition today's rock players have received. Nonetheless, its a very intriguing style that has limitless capabilities. Witness the incredible playing of Stanley Jordan, who *never* picks a note! He juxtaposes melodies played by his tapping right hand while the left hand taps on full chords. Many times he'll combine the two for incredible single-note runs that are only possible within this technique. Of course, this is the most attractive feature of this style—the ability to play certain note and chord combinations that are not possible in the standard left- and right-hand roles.

Proper Tapping Techniques

We must be aware before attempting to use this technique that we are actually creating an entirely new note with a finger on the right hand, in a similar way that we learned in the hammer-on section. This means that extreme accuracy and a lot of strength are required within a short distance. This is particularly true since we are making many of these right-handed hammer-ons in some rather tight spaces up on the thinner high frets.

To begin let's take a look at some very simple tap-on licks with photos to help you see exactly what is happening. In this example, we see how the right-handed hammer-on can directly follow a standard left-handed hammer-on, thereby making a stretch that would be almost impossible under normal circumstances.

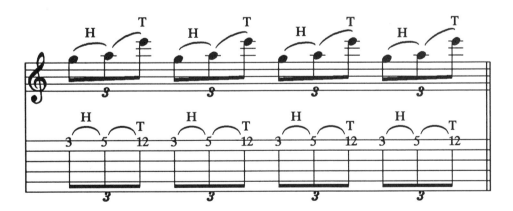

Placing a right-handed hammer-on after a string is bent is another great use of tapping, but remember, the tapped-on note is now affected just as the original bent note was. The exciting thing now is that you can bend, hammer-on, and then release the bend while the higher note is still depressed creating some very interesting melodic possibilities:

Contemporary Heavy Metal Guitar

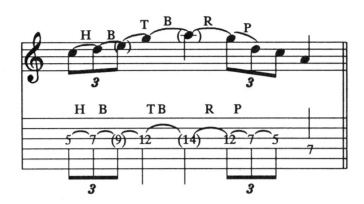

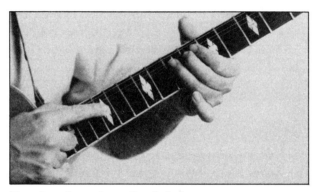

Tapping the string after it is bent.

You can also continue to tap-on with other fingers of the right hand, as in this example, where we actually use the index finger and the ring finger to create a very long, extended tap-on.

Continuous tapping by both hands on the same string.

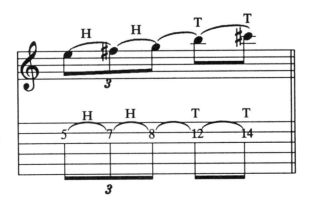

Contemporary Heavy Metal Guitar

In many cases, the tapping hand also acts as the pulling–off device that creates more notes *after* it has done a tap-on. This requires even more stability from the right hand. Grabbing the sides of the fingerboard adds support and helps the right hand maintain a stronger and steadier position as shown in the photo below. Note that in this exercise we are shifting the tapped-on note as well as its pull-off position. We must keep shifting these positions while holding onto the sides of the neck as a continued guide and support for these pull-offs.

Position for right-hand hammer-ons, or "tapping," and pulling off.

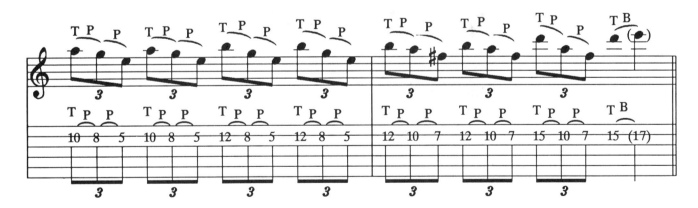

Many of the flashier tap-on specialists such as Eddie Van Halen, Allan Holdsworth, and Steve Vai employ a rapid succession of tap-ons and pull-offs on a series of strings that usually repeat a pattern. This is a difficult technique to play quickly as it requires a tremendous amount of accuracy within relatively tight quarters. Proceed carefully with this one at first—slowly building up speed as your technique improves.

Contemporary Heavy Metal Guitar

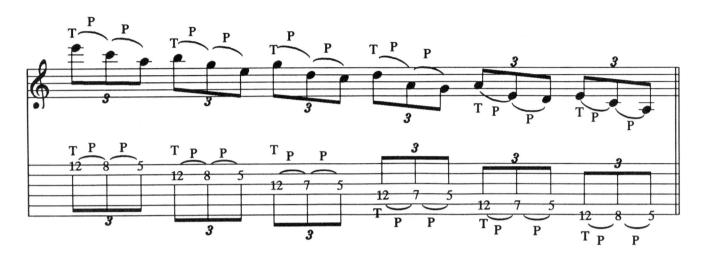

Perhaps the most acrobatic of all the tap-on techniques is the formation of a new chord position from a series of notes played on a group of strings with an arpeggiated group of tap-ons over the original notes. This is a very difficult technique, and you really have to know where you're going and where you're coming from when attempting it. Its even harder to execute if you grow the nails of your right hand long for fingerpicking, as they would tend to accidentally hit other strings as well as your designated target strings.

Two tapped arpeggios, three notes each.

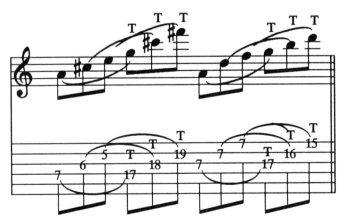

Yet another tap-on technique is one in which the right hand actually crosses over to fret notes that are lower than the notes played by the left hand. In this way it acts as a very secure "anchor" that we can create alternating hammer-ons and pull-offs over. This is a slightly easier technique than some of the other tap-ons because it enables you to use the left hand, which is more accustomed to hammers and pulls and is at a better angle for this task, Note how we can move the anchored right-hand note for some interesting effects.

Positions for two-handed hammer-pull.

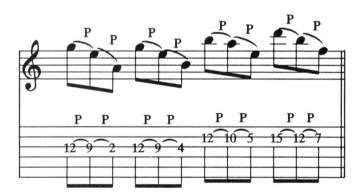

Vivian Campbell, of Whitesnake and Dio Fame, showed me an interesting technique that has the right hand muting the strings below a hammer-on and pull-off lick that is being played with the left hand. Although this technique does look flashy, the right hand does not serve to *play* any notes; it simply acts to dampen the strings and to keep them from causing any extraneous noise.

Contemporary Heavy Metal Guitar

Dampening the strings with right-hand grab.

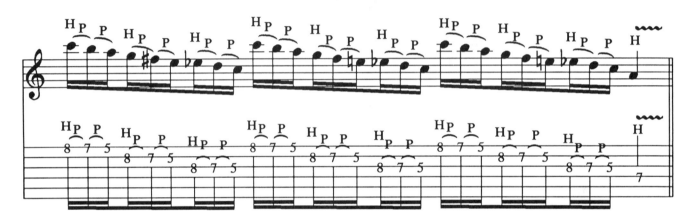

Vivian Campbell.
Photo: Arlen Roth.

You can use two fingers to tap-on two notes simultaneously as in the following example, creating a full chord with the notes hammered-on by the left hand.

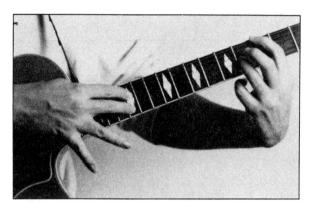

Two two-note chords being tapped by both hands.

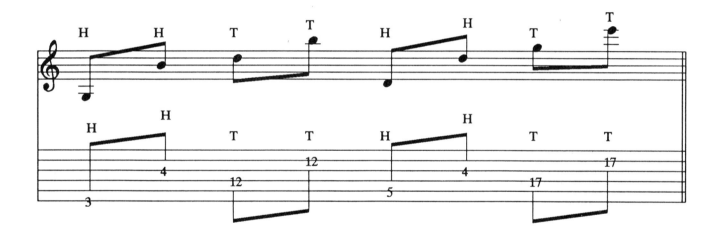

Harmonic Tap-ons

Creating harmonics with tap-ons is something that has been unique to my style for many years, and I've never seen it done anywhere else. In this technique, we simply play a note that is fretted, give it good sustain, then lightly tap-on a harmonic to that note precisely twelve frets above it. There are, of course, many other harmonic relationships you can tap-on, but the twelve-fret octave is the strongest one to use in this case. Remember, since we are creating harmonics we must tap directly over the metal fret itself, then quickly remove it as soon as the harmonic starts to ring. Once it is ringing, some vibrato will help the sustaining quality of the harmonic and further distinguish it from the original octave note. The examples that follow show some of the various possibilities within this intriguing style, such as bending the note after the harmonic tap-on, two-note harmonics, and split-harmonics. Hope you enjoy them!

140

Contemporary Heavy Metal Guitar

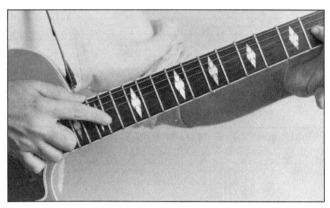

A "harmonic" tap-on.

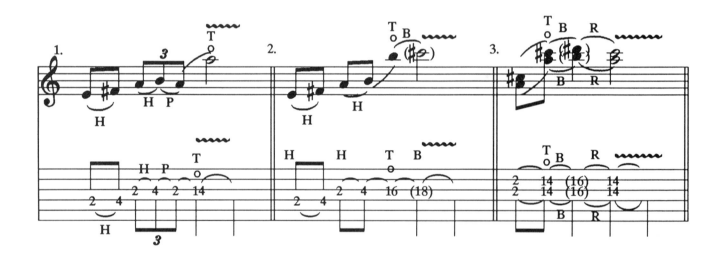

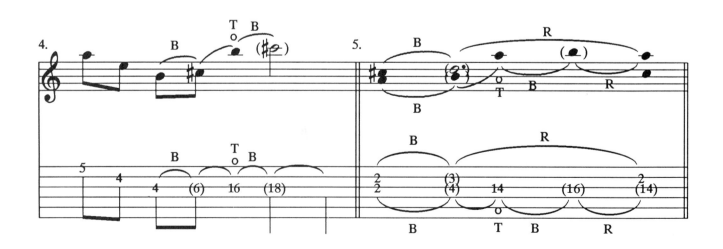

Contemporary Heavy Metal Guitar

That's about all the tap-on possibilities I can think of, so now let's put them to work! This first solo is in the style of Eddie Van Halen, and combines rapid single-note work with an occasional use of tapping for a dramatic effect. You'll find that in the long run this dramatic style is perhaps the most common use for right-hand tapping.

Sammy Hagar and Eddie Van Halen.
© Ebet Roberts, 1986.

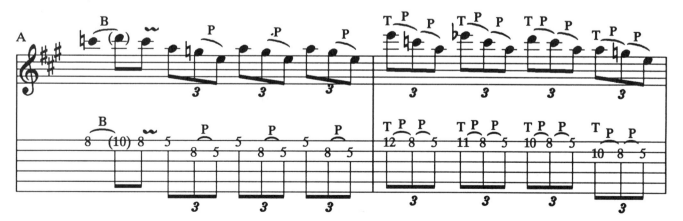

Contemporary Heavy Metal Guitar

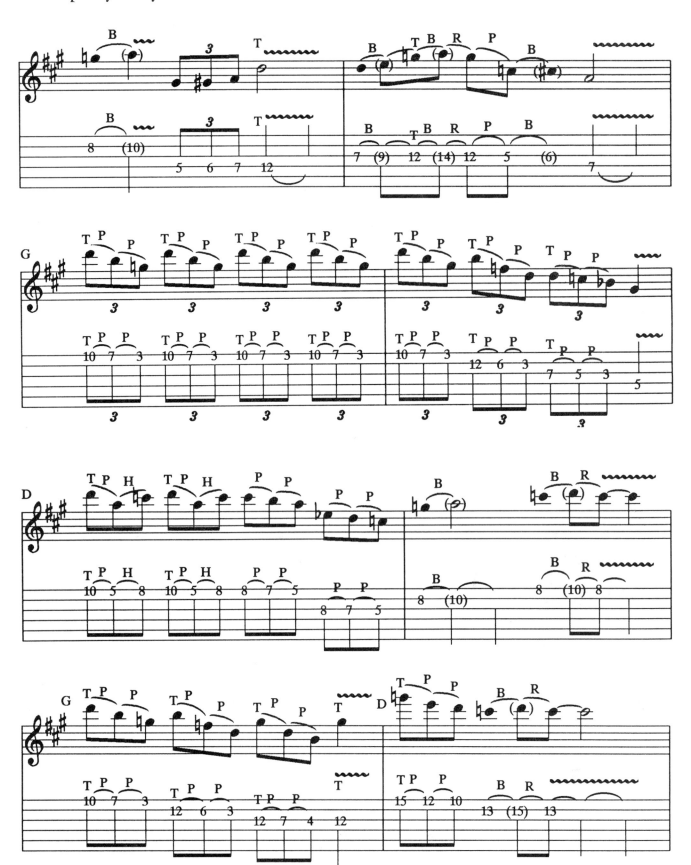

Contemporary Heavy Metal Guitar

The next solo piece employs the tapping approach across many strings, creating some very dramatic and exciting cascading runs. All of these combine the right-handed taps with left-handed pull-offs.

Jake E. Lee of the Ozzy Osbourne Band.
© Ebet Roberts, 1986.

Contemporary Heavy Metal Guitar

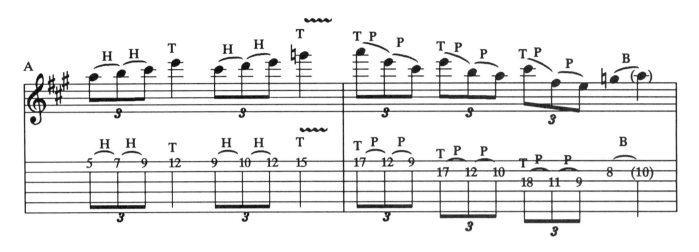

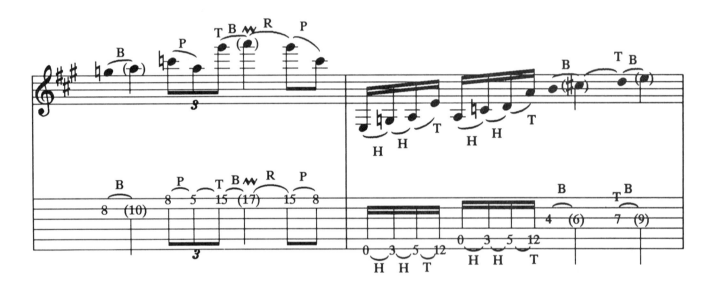

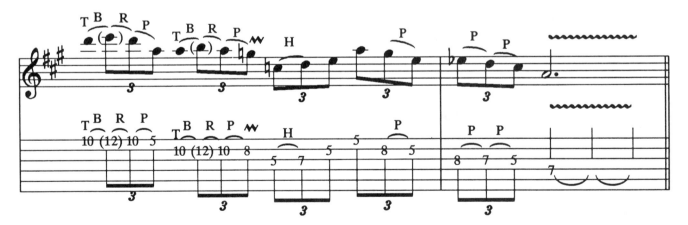

Next is a solo piece designed to make use of the harmonic tap-ons I discussed earlier. Note that we're using both single and double-note harmonics, as well as bending them often after the harmonic has occurred. These can be used to greatly enhance the emotion of your more powerful solos.

Contemporary Heavy Metal Guitar

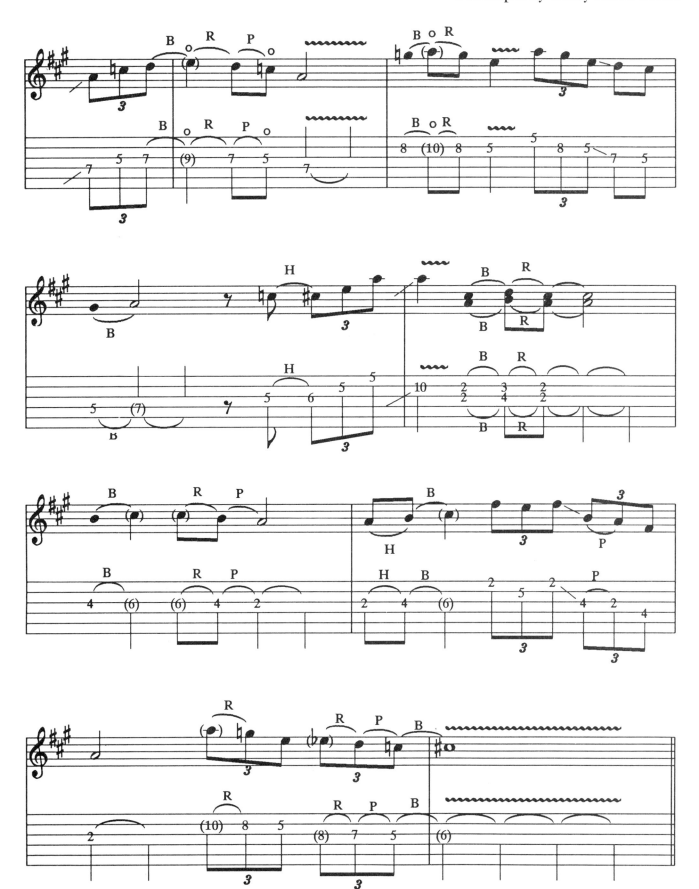

Contemporary Heavy Metal Guitar

This final tap-on piece pulls out all the stops in the sense that absolutely *nothing* is picked. We must, à la Stanley Jordan, derive all of our notes from hammer-ons or tap-ons by both hands. This will require some getting used to, especially when it comes to getting equal strength and sustain out of all of them. Notice that for the most part we are reserving the bottom strings for the left hand, while the right hand handles the "lead" tapping on the higher strings.

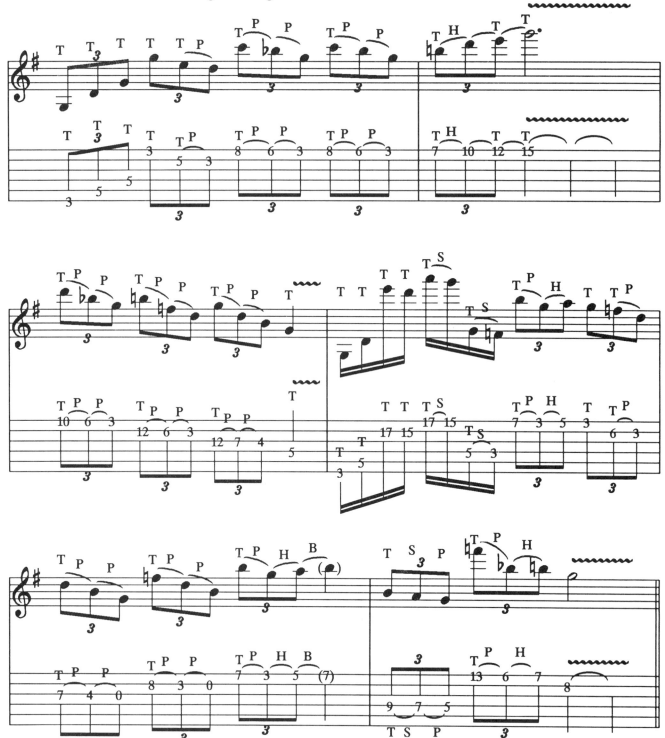

Steve Vai: A Contemporary Metal Master

Steve Vai is one of heavy metal guitar's brightest stars. He is currently at the top, playing with Whitesnake, after playing for years with David Lee Roth, Frank Zappa, and Alcatrazz (where he replaced Yngwie Malmsteen). He has also done work on film scores and with Yoko Ono. He is a player without peer as far as technique and style are concerned, and in a time when many guitarists are being cloned, he stands as a monument to originality and individual expression. I personally got to meet and work with Steve on the set of the movie, *Crossroads*, in which he played the devilish Jack Butler, the man my student, Ralph Macchio (of *Karate Kid* fame), must guitar duel with at the film's finale.

Steve Vai is a player who not only sounds brilliant technically, but uses all of that technique to get out what's inside emotionally. This is perhaps what separates him most of all from his heavy metal peers, many of whom seem to be just running through scale after scale, with little or no improvisational character to their work.

Director Walter Hill (left), Arlen Roth, and Steve Vai (right) on the set of *Crossroads*.
Photo: Stephen Vaughan.

Besides the typical blues and pentatonic scales, Steve likes to improvise with the Dorian and Lydian modes. He sees them mainly as "flavors" as opposed to theoretical notes, though he did first learn them perfectly with many hours of practice *before* he started to let them take on that character in his playing. Now he feels that he can simply hear the Dorian sound, for example, and his fingers will go right to it. This is the kind of spontaneity you should look for in your playing as well, but it will only come after putting in lots of time with your guitar. Steve believes that once these scales are truly memorized, soon only the sound of the mode is left as the rest of the scale seems to fall away into less importance. In his opinion, ear training is the single most important aspect of becoming a musician, because with trained ears, you have more to choose from, hence more to express your feelings and imagination with. It's better to have the ability to express what's inside rather than simply fall back on overly developed "chops." He emphasizes that chops (i.e., great technical prowess) *are* an important expressive outlet, but that ear training is what brings out the best songwriting capabilities.

Steve is least concerned with the mechanics of playing when performing in front of an audience. He worries about mechanics when he's practicing at home. When in front of the crowd the focus must be on the performance aspect, since that's when all your knowledge is put to the test and there are no second chances.

The communication between you and the people alters the way in which you approach your instrument. Compared to when you play alone, your ears act differently, your fingers act differently, and even your *legs* act differently when you are performing! Steve feels that when he played with David Lee Roth his playing got somewhat better, but more significantly his expression on the instrument was completely different, because for the most part people were there to be *entertained*. The musical subtleties of what was played were translated by a very select few in the crowd. In fact Steve had to concentrate on just playing the notes, since he would run around so much on stage! Because he played in large arenas (where the sound tends to carry in some very strange ways) he could play a flurry of notes and it would go unnoticed, whereas if he threw the guitar up in the air and caught it on the right chord, he'd make much more of an impression! So as you can see, playing as fast as you can in an arena can be meaningless, whereas the expression on your instrument and your showmanship are what really count.

Steve is a teacher as well as a professional player, and has seen a wide variety of student types. He found that some learned more when instructed on a strictly mechanical level, while others were better with technical or emotional approaches. Each student is a unique musical entity, and it's good for the young player to acquire a healthy balance mechanical, technical, and emotional musicianship. For Steve, being a musician isn't simply "playing from the heart" but possessing the technical and mechanical skills to provide the added freedom needed for all of this expression. In his words, "If you knew a lot more music, your heart would also speak better, and if you have the technical ability behind you, and don't let it get too carried away with itself, the emotional aspects will be very much enhanced." This is hard to understand when you're growing up, and it's very difficult to stress during these days of techno-wizardry on the guitar.

Steve also feels that whether a player has limited skills or is a true master, he or she is always "one" with the instrument. It doesn't really matter whether the player is copying someone else or creating original style, the way the instrument is played always says something about the *player* and his or her relationship to the instrument. He admits that when he was growing up and playing in bands he was actually *closer* to the instrument than he is now. A lot of the pressure of being on top is that it can "fool around with your head," especially in the sense that you feel you must always do a certain degree of "impressing," even though you're already fully accepted for your own individuality.

Steve also believes that it's really hard to teach people anything unless they are truly inspired by their teacher, as he was so lucky to have been during his years as a developing player.

Steve agrees that it's very important to understand the "roots" of what you're into playing in order to know what has come before you. Although he has really only studied as far back as Jeff Beck, Jimi Hendrix, and Jimmy Page, by studying them in a sense he studied all that *they* had absorbed before they rose to prominence.

Steve advises that it is a mistake to excessively worship any one player, because you'll be limiting and "pigeonholing" yourself. There are some things you *can* do to help develop your own style on the instrument. The first thing is to realize that you *do* have your own sound that can come forth on your instrument. You must *convince* yourself that you truly believe that: *"There's me, and there's nobody else!"* Quite simply put, Steve believes that if you keep aware of this at all times, you'll be able to recognize what is derivative and what lacks originality in your playing.

As far as specific exercises are concerned, particularly ones that *you* can help develop, this next idea is a good one for developing all three aspects of your playing: mechanical, technical, and emotional. It requires a great deal of discipline, but that's often the name of the game if you really want to improve. Play any two notes, and *only* those two notes, for an hour each time you practice. Once you've choosen them, try to play them in every possible way, in every conceivable location on the neck. After just a few minutes, you'll be forced to stretch your imagination just to make it through the sheer monotony of playing only these two notes! The following is an exercise based upon this principle that only scratches the surface of the kinds of things Steve is talking about. I wrote it out to give you an idea of how *I* would experiment with this exercise in the hope of inspiring you to work out some of your ideas.

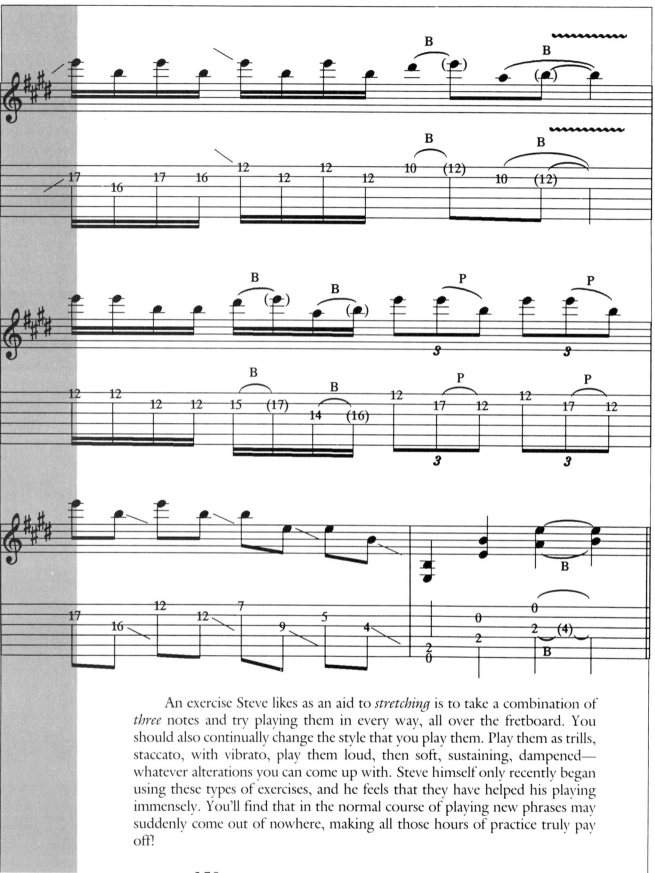

An exercise Steve likes as an aid to *stretching* is to take a combination of *three* notes and try playing them in every way, all over the fretboard. You should also continually change the style that you play them. Play them as trills, staccato, with vibrato, play them loud, then soft, sustaining, dampened—whatever alterations you can come up with. Steve himself only recently began using these types of exercises, and he feels that they have helped his playing immensely. You'll find that in the normal course of playing new phrases may suddenly come out of nowhere, making all those hours of practice truly pay off!

When asked about some of the more unusual and creative ways he practiced during his formative years, Steve recalled a game he would play with his other teenage guitar-playing friends to help train his ear. He would lie down with his eyes closed and have a friend finger a chord—*any* chord. He would then call out what colors and shapes the chord sounded like to him. Then he tried to name the chord by listening closely to the intervals within it. This way, he'd end up with not only the name of a chord, but also its whole character as well. Steve felt that this was a great exercise because it was enormous fun and it helped him develop a creative understanding of the guitar and music in general. It also had the added benefit of keeping him close with his friends in a creative atmosphere. Now that Steve has begun to write music for film, he is really seeing the benefits of this early game, since he must look at a picture and come up with sound to describe or complement *it!*

Steve Vai is a true rock and roll master, and one who is as concerned with helping younger players as he is with his own incredible career. You can find him these days on the road and in the studio with the supergroup, Whitesnake; he has also released a solo album of great complexity and power called *Passion and Warfare*. If you get a chance to see him, don't miss it—he's a one of a kind guitarist in a world of musical sameness.

The following are two of Steve's extraordinary solos from the David Lee Roth album, *Eat 'Em and Smile*. They are from the songs "Elephant Gun" and "Goin' Crazy" and represent heavy metal lead guitar at its finest. Take note of Vai's subtle use of various techniques; and I also suggest getting the record so you can hear exactly how these pieces have been executed.

"Elephant Gun" Solo, transcribed by John Frusciante

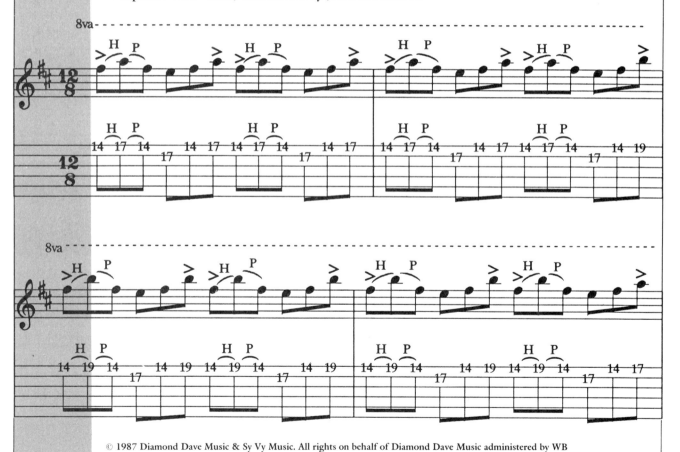

© 1987 Diamond Dave Music & Sy Vy Music. All rights on behalf of Diamond Dave Music administered by WB Music Corp. All rights reserved. Used by permission.

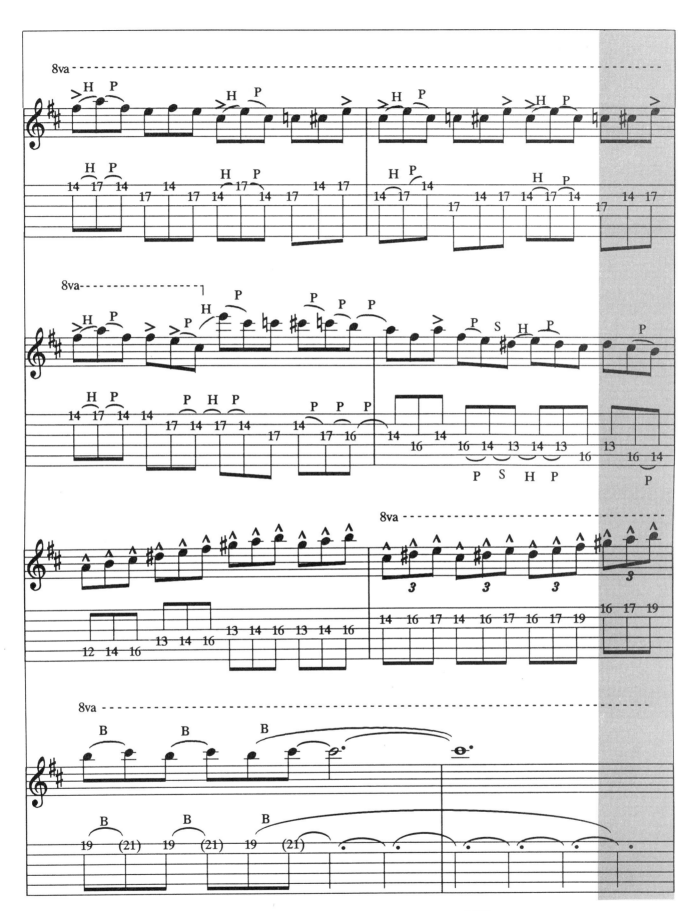

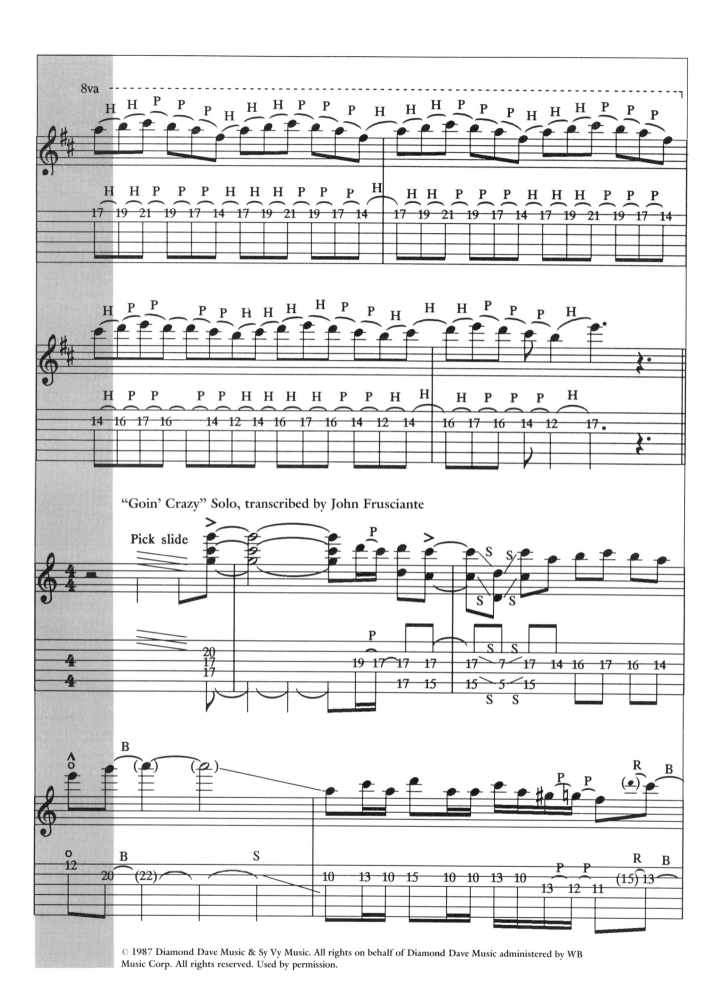

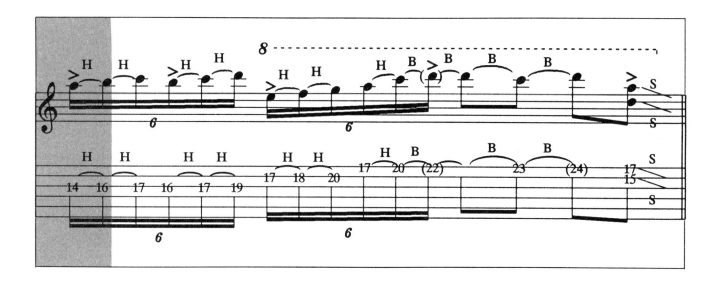

EIGHT

Double and Harmony Guitar Soloing

Musicians have always enjoyed playing in unison or in harmony with each other. This is very evident in the fiddle-and-mandolin combinations of Bluegrass music, as well as the guitar and clarinet of the big band sound. Two musicians playing in perfect unison or harmony is a special skill, like two tapdancers working out their routines together.

Doubled or harmony guitar parts are nothing new. There were many teams that specialized in this style during the 1930s and 1940s, especially in the jazz format. Unison and harmony lead rock guitar playing really began to catch on during the southern-rock invasion of the early 1970s. The most notable and influential dual guitar players were Duane Allman and Dickey Betts of The Allman Brothers Band, along with groups such as Lynyrd Skynyrd, The Marshall Tucker Band, and Black Oak Arkansas. These groups featured solos that gradually built up from one guitarist to two, first playing lines in unison, then in two-part harmony. This became a trademark of the southern-rock sound, and for several years was its most identifiable "hook."

Doubled and harmony guitar parts have since been adopted by many heavy metal groups, almost as a "refinement" of what might be a rather untamed sound. It tends to give more of an air of organization and "arrangement," especially when one becomes used to hearing improvised solos. The very concept of a prearranged, orderly solo in heavy metal may seem strange, but it works. Many groups have used the two-guitar attack successfully, such as The Scorpions, Iron Maiden, and most notably Night Ranger's Brad Gillis and Jeff Watson. In heavy metal there is more emphasis on players taking solos than in the days of southern-rock, yet unison playing and harmony runs are still effectively and tastefully used.

The first group of exercises is to get you used to the concept of unison and harmony lines. You'll note that I've dispensed with the standard notation, replacing it with two lines of tablature on top of each other to illustrate the two simultaneous guitar parts. Play through each part (especially if you don't have someone to harmonize with) and take special note of where these harmonies lie in relation to each other.

Double and Harmony Guitar Soloing

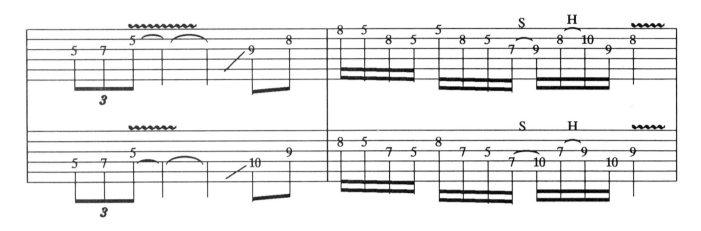

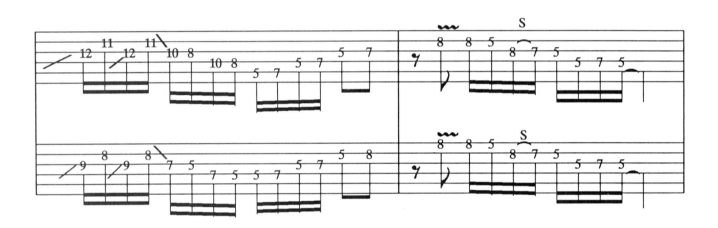

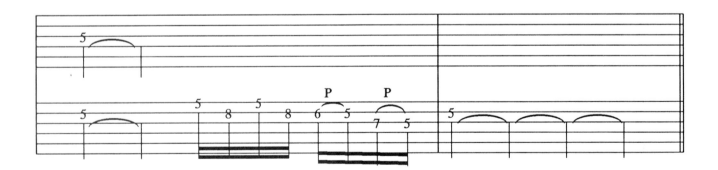

Here are some harmony runs that use bending as a major part of the process. The notes you choose to bend in harmony must be very carefully chosen, and the act of bending and how long it takes to reach the peak of the bend must be well-synchronized with the other guitarist to enhance the two-guitar effect.

Double and Harmony Guitar Soloing

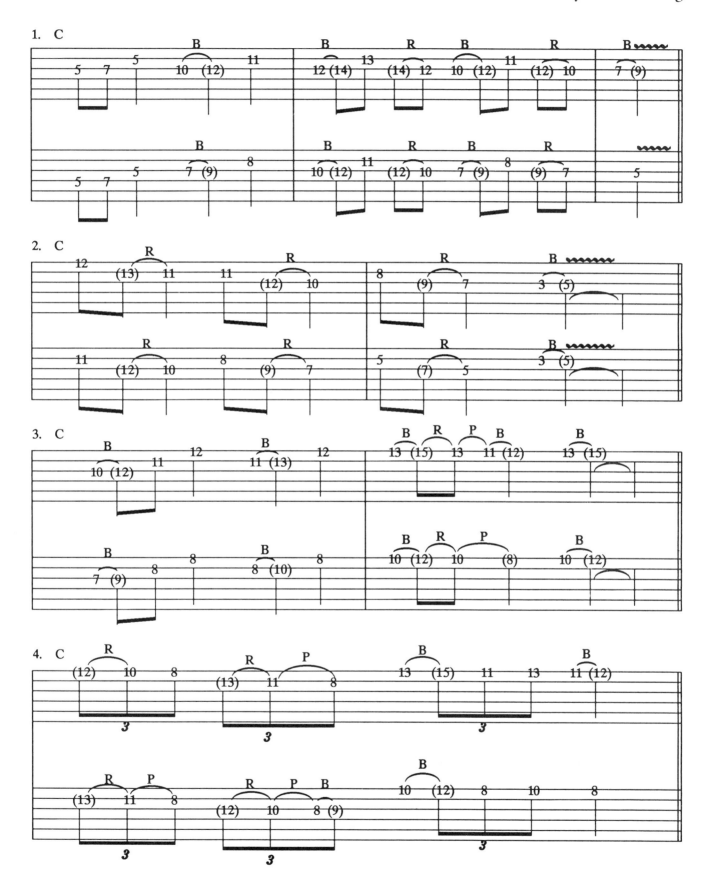

Double and Harmony Guitar Soloing

Moving more into the contemporary heavy metal vein, we see how the two-guitar harmony technique can be used in explosive, rapid single-note runs. In order to discover harmony parts to runs that you already know, start the same run only three notes later, almost in a "row, row, row your boat" fashion. This will not only create a harmony to the original run, but also an echo-like effect with the repeat of notes just heard from the other guitar part. Here are a few runs illustrating this approach—some are harmonizing in thirds, while others harmonize in fourths and fifths.

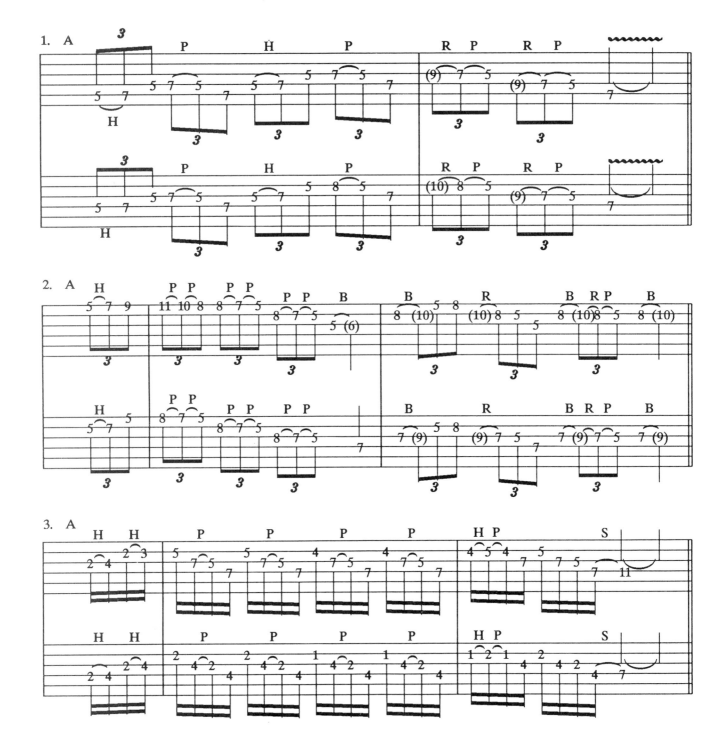

▲ 161

Double and Harmony Guitar Soloing

Right-hand tapping is a very dynamic style when used in a two-guitar format, and can be a very acrobatic technique to use in front of an audience. What the audience will not realize, however, is that this is easier than trying to harmonize complex single-note runs. This is mainly due to the fact that although the licks in right-handed hammers hold their positions more often, they tend to hold the interest of the listener because of their stylistic nature.

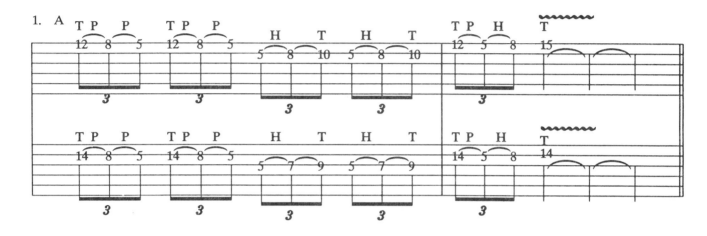

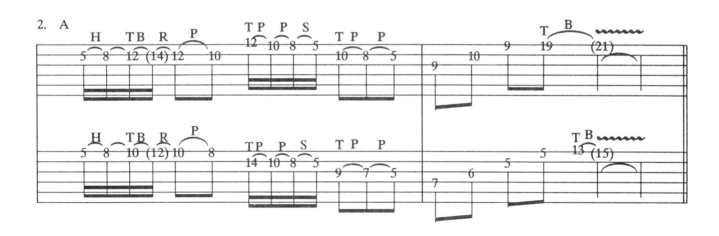

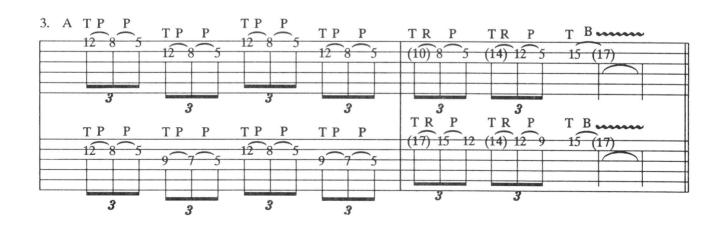

Arpeggiating Your Solos

Arpeggiation is a very useful way of creating new single-note runs from positions not usually associated with scale work. An **arpeggio** is a note-by-note line that is created from an existing chord position. With this technique we can create some very interesting single-note lines from thinking in terms of "shapes" on the fretboard, rather than the more scholarly scales we've gotten used to practicing.

To further solidify the concept of what an arpeggio is, here are some simple exercises that show some arpeggiated chords played in a deliberate fashion.

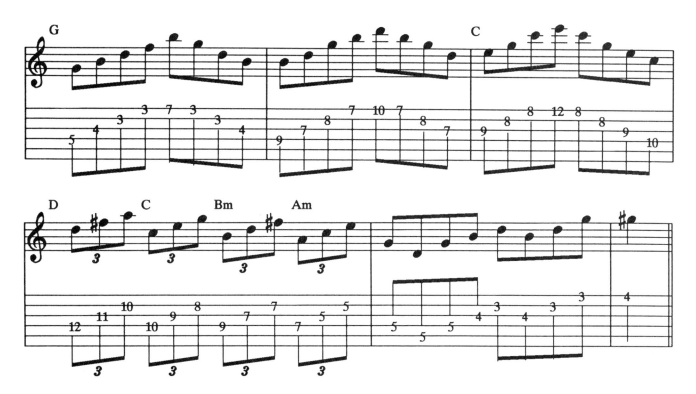

Arpeggiating Your Solos

Some arpeggio licks can move in the opposite direction—starting on the higher strings, and then moving to the lower ones such as the licks that follow. Make sure to begin these exercises with an upstroke of the pick—this will get your hand flowing in the proper direction for the remainder of the run.

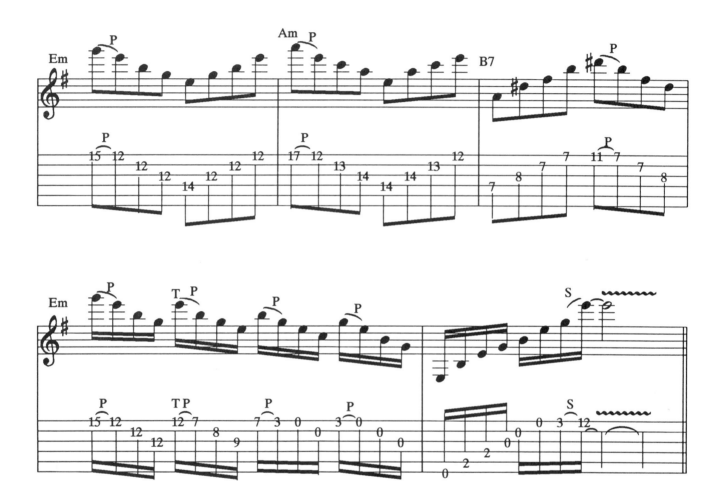

As you continue to build up speed with these types of runs, the previsualization of the notes to be arpeggiated must take shape more quickly in your mind. Many times they are not necessarily chords so much as they are "shapes" of connecting notes that fall easily and conveniently underneath your fingertips. Below are some more advanced arpeggio licks in this vein. Remember that you should only keep the notes down as long as needed for the lick to sound, then you should quickly release them to add to the run's very important single-note flow. It's far better to make these sound like real patterns rather than just chords that have been "dragged" across.

▲ 165

Arpeggiating Your Solos

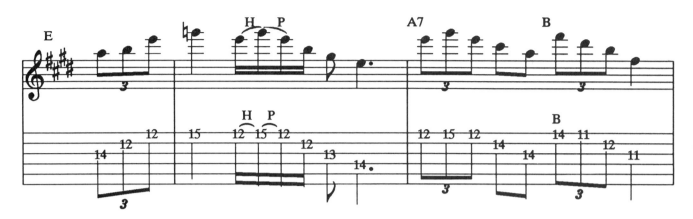

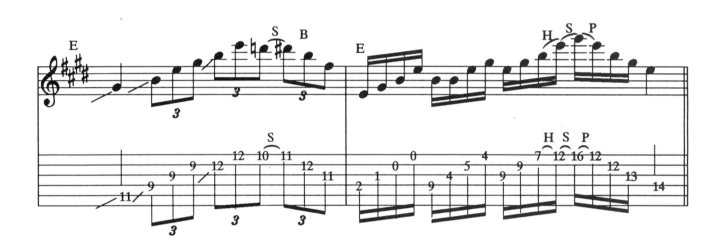

This last group of licks utilizes arpeggios that move in both directions—towards the high E string, and away from it. Note that in some instances we are actually combining these directions over the course of just one lick, making for some pretty fancy picking technique! I hope you enjoy them!

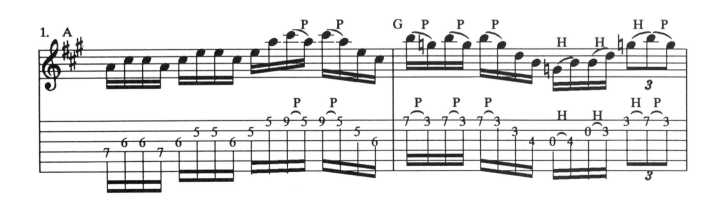

Arpeggiating Your Solos

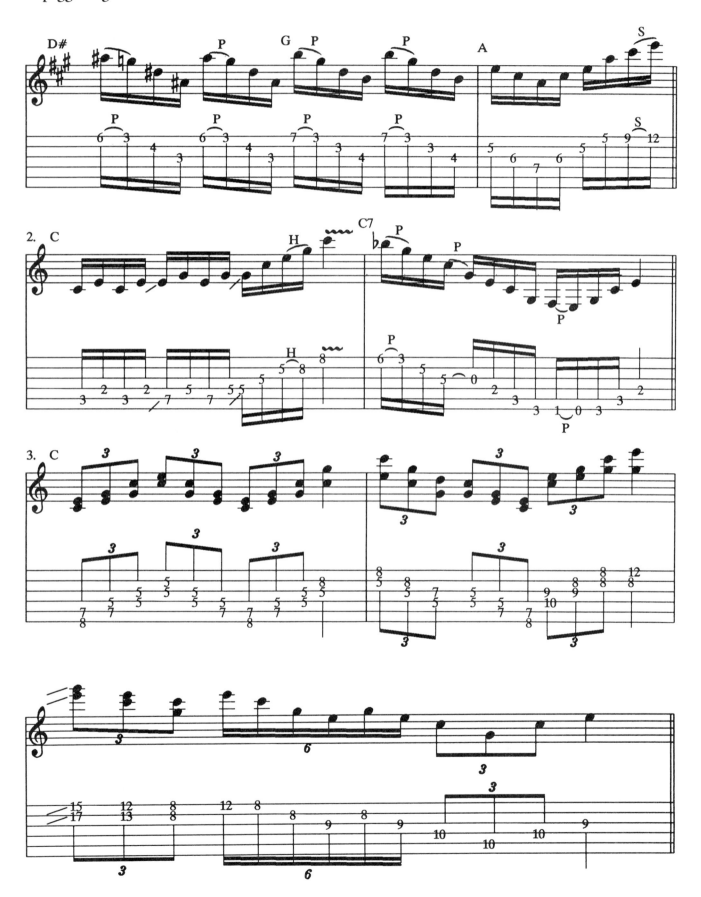

▲ 167

Arpeggiating Your Solos

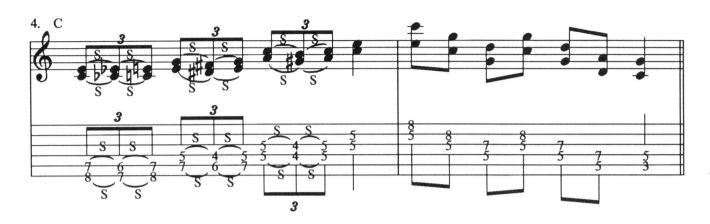

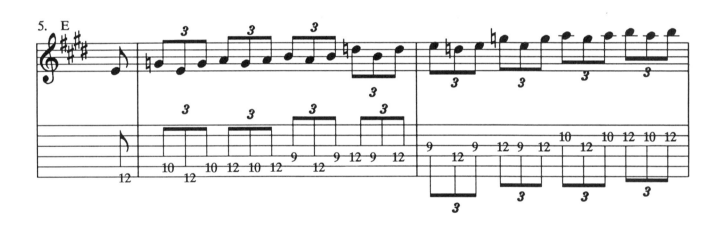

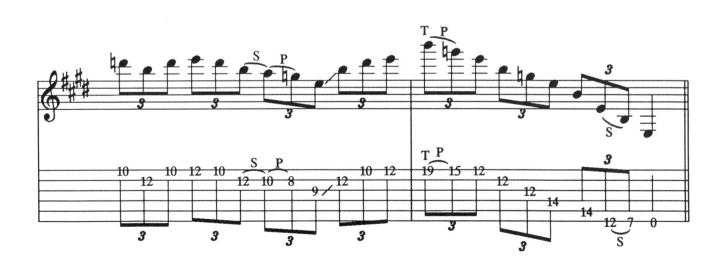

MODAL ARPEGGIOS

The use of arpeggios in heavy metal guitar playing has reached epic proportions, and no doubt points to the influence that classical music now has over it. By taking a particular mode and playing the scale degrees 1, 3, 5, 7, 9, 11, 13, a modal arpeggio is achieved, and it sounds like we're playing a seven-note chord. The following group of modal arpeggios can be used in many soloing situations, and can be heard in the playing styles of Steve Vai, Vinnie Moore, and Joe Satriani. Note that while these are all written out in D, starting on the fifth fret of the A string, they can happen all over the neck. Try to find the other positions and practice them as well.

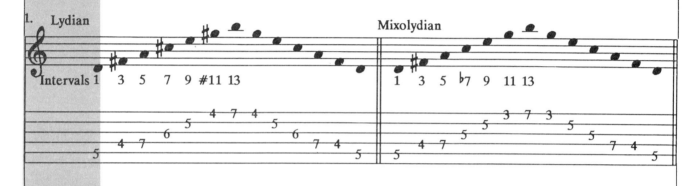

TWO-HANDED TAPPING ARPEGGIOS

Perhaps the ultimate contemporary heavy metal style to master is the combination of Van Halen-style right-hand tapping *with* an arpeggio sound. This is best achieved by adding straight left-handed hammer-ons and pull-offs. When properly executed, this technique can give you a very smooth, clean sound that has great clarity and articulation even at very high volumes. I've written out two groups of exercises here, one for ascending arpeggios and one for descending. These can make for very exciting musical moments, and can do a lot for your soloing.

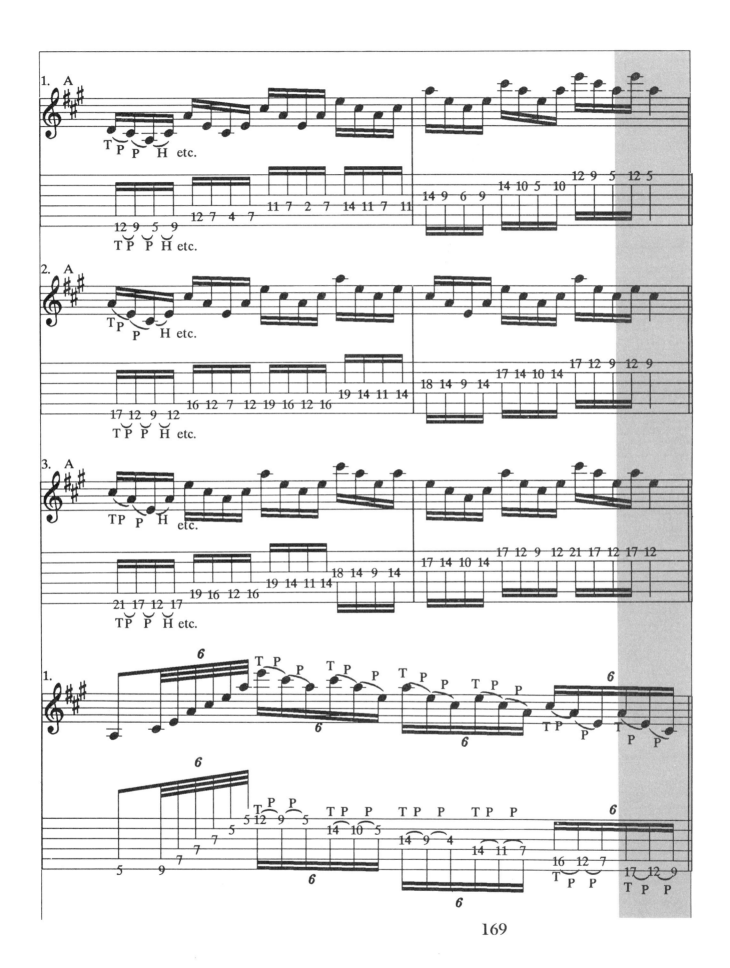

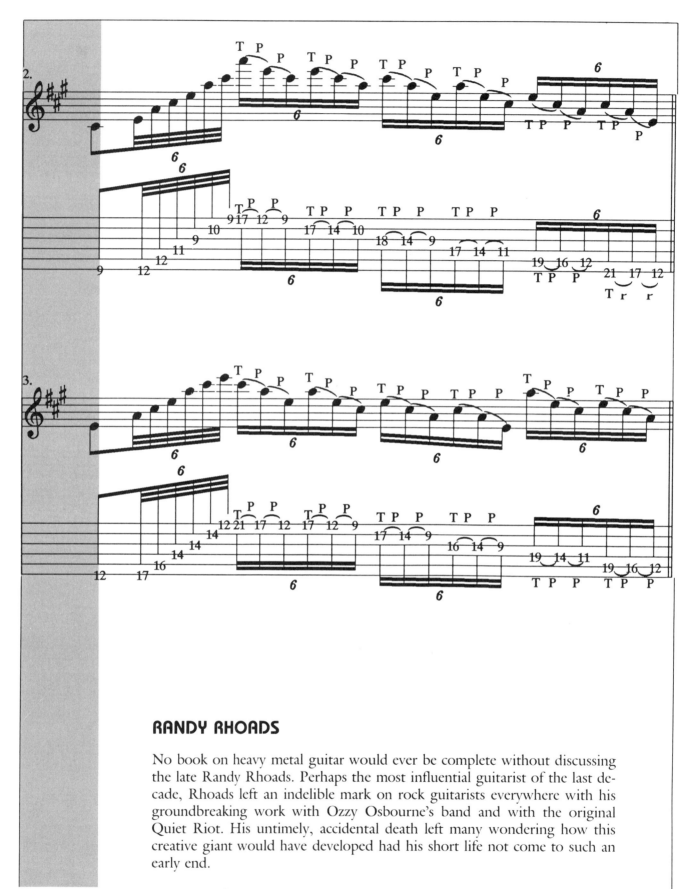

RANDY RHOADS

No book on heavy metal guitar would ever be complete without discussing the late Randy Rhoads. Perhaps the most influential guitarist of the last decade, Rhoads left an indelible mark on rock guitarists everywhere with his groundbreaking work with Ozzy Osbourne's band and with the original Quiet Riot. His untimely, accidental death left many wondering how this creative giant would have developed had his short life not come to such an early end.

A guitarist with deep classical influences, Rhoads led the way for the classically influenced metal soloing that is so prevalent today. This influence was perhaps most clearly displayed through his left-hand technique. Flavored with huge doses of hammer-ons and pull-offs, Rhoads' left-hand created a beautiful legato sound which is still trying to be captured by many of today's rock guitarists. He played mainly in the Aeolian mode, many times with the pentatonic blues scales thrown in as well. For this section, I've taken excerpts from some of his most memorable Ozzy solos to illustrate his legato and modal approach. These are from three songs: "Over the Mountain," "You Can't Kill Rock 'N Roll," and "Believer"—perhaps the one solo that most clearly illustrates his use of the pentatonic blues scale.

Be sure to pay close attention to all of the left-handed subtleties. Achieving the truly legato effect will probably take a while, but you'll find all the work to be worth it in the long run!

Randy Rhoads.
© Jon Sievert, 1989.

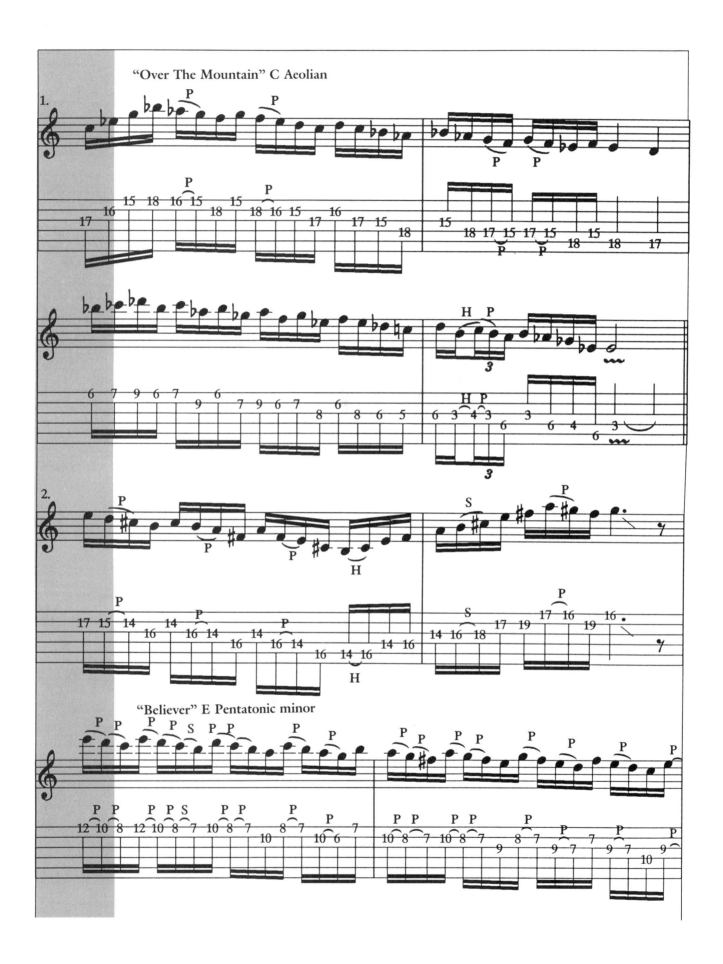

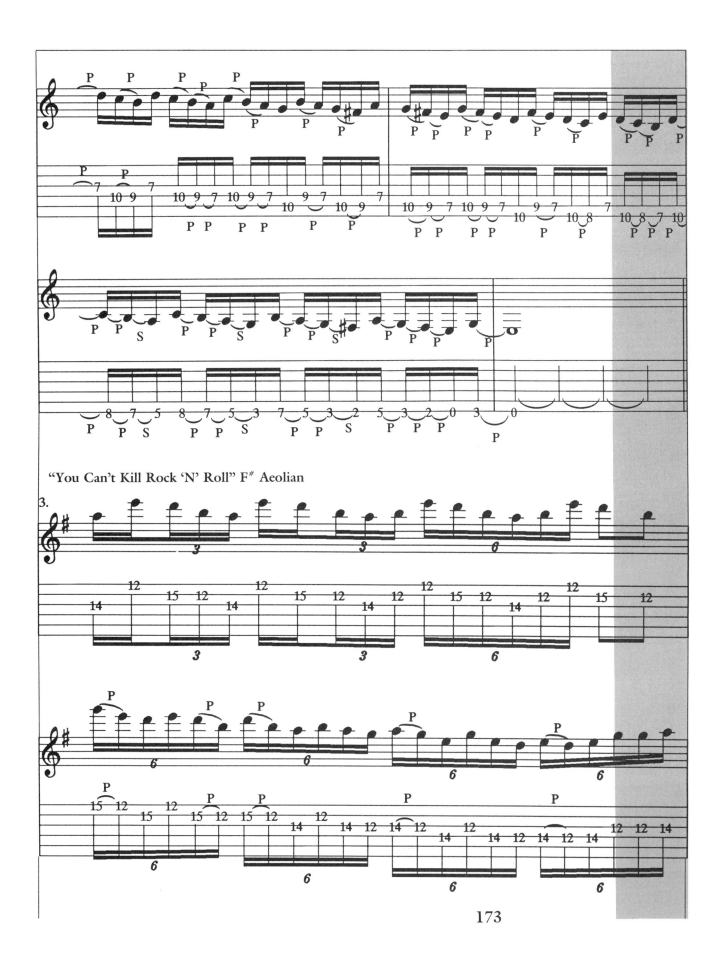

"You Can't Kill Rock 'N' Roll" F# Aeolian

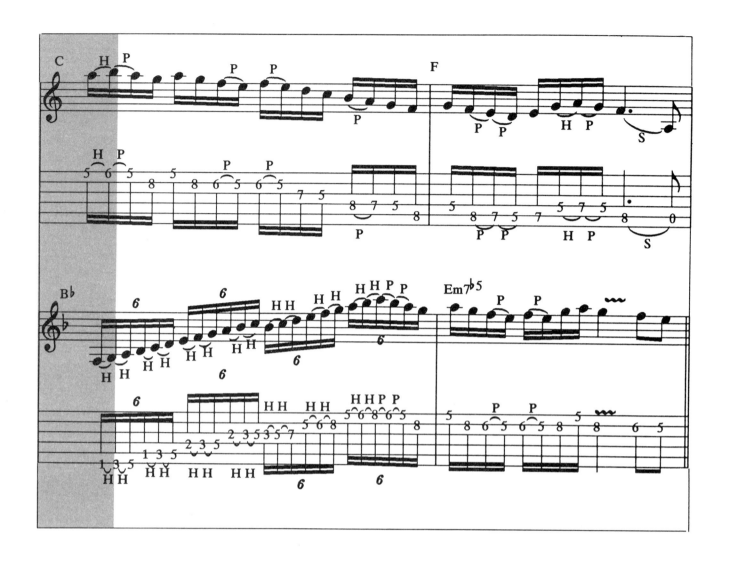

Forming and Working with a Band

Now you may feel that you've practiced enough by yourself, and that you're confident that it's time to start the long process of forming a band and hopefully recording and "making it!" Take my word for it, this *is* a long, hard road. However, if you have the drive, ambition, talent, and if you have fun doing all of this, you stand a good chance of getting somewhere.

With heavy metal's booming popularity, a group needn't come from one of the major metropolitan areas to make it big. There are definitely enough heavy metal fans to go around, and that goes for England, Germany, and many other foreign countries as well as the United States. Just look at how many successful groups have come from these nations and made it big in the States!

Of course, the first and perhaps most important step is to find the right musicians to play with. Most metal bands consist of a lead singer, bass, drums, synthesizer, and two guitars; but any smaller combination of this format can work. Many musicians "double" on another instrument and can help the band's overall sound and performance with this versatility. Check out Eddie Van Halen's occasional synthesizer work—played with the guitar still hanging from his shoulders. If you have a little keyboard knowledge you could take it a long way in this manner.

Generally speaking, the music world is rather small, and musicians tend to seek each other out eventually. The key is to let yourself and your talents be *known*. At first this may mean going to your local music store, asking for a guitar, and proceeding to play so hot that everybody has to take notice! I recall, how I used to walk self-assuredly into the intimidating atmosphere of New York's 48th Street music shops, ask for one of the best guitars in the shop, sit down, and proceed to give a *performance!*

This convinced me that what I thought sounded great in my living room was really as good as I thought since other people were attracted to the sounds that I was making. Before I knew it, I was giving my phone number to many interested musicians! Even if you live in a small town, the same thing can happen to you. More than likely, the people who work in the store are musicians as well, and they will surely take notice of you if you've really "got it."

School is another place to meet musicians, as kids with similar interests tend to "hang out" with each other. That's how I formed my first band at the age of eleven, and also how The Beatles met too!

If there are any local bands you admire, and if you want them to take notice of you, by all means go to their shows or rehearsals and introduce yourself. See if you can get them to let you jam with them. Unfortunately, this is a time when many musicians fall prey to attitudes that are not always conducive to building up one's confidence. Many small-time players who've had a taste of success at an early age—and "success" can be anything from a recording contract on down to simply impressing the right girl—will make it very difficult for aspiring, less-experienced players to get even the right time of day from them. This is all a very childish but take my word for it: if you're good, and they hear you, your playing will speak for itself. Before you know it, *they'll* be the ones trying to get to know *you!*

Many areas have regional newspapers that cater to local bands and musicians. These are good places to advertise for other musicians or to look for ads to answer yourself. They're also good for looking for used guitars and other equipment. Believe me, it's very important to try to save money in this department, especially if you're just starting out.

REHEARSING

Once you've found the people you think will make up a good band, or even if you have just one other musician to play with, it's important that you establish some kind of disciplined schedule for rehearsing together. Obviously, if you have a paying job that is forthcoming, rehearsal is a necessity, but even if you're just jamming together in hopes of one day working as a band, it's important to fuel your enthusiasm by playing together often. Playing together frequently will also make you "tighter" as a band, and will fine-tune your musical communications. It will also expose any flaws a certain player might have, and will help in the evolution of the band until it has all the right players doing the right things.

Heavy metal is a very theatrical form of music these days, and many of today's biggest bands do a lot of rehearsing with walls of mirrors in front of them so they can synchronize their moves. This is all great, and I hope you strive to be a flamboyant performer as well, but don't forget the basics first. Get the music to be where *you* want it and don't be satisfied until it's right. Only then should you start seriously working on making your show visually unique.

Again, beware of clashes of ego. These can be the source of great struggles within a group, but if musically motivated, can make for an atmosphere of electrically charged creativity. Musicians' fragile personalities sometimes become quite artistically sensitive. Ironically, the groups that have musical arguments are often the most successful! It's best to think of the band as one person, and that person as having some inner conflicts during the creation of a work of art. This truly is the case and believing it will help you get through some of the hard emotional times.

More often than not, the lead guitarist of a band is looked to for leadership. This is no accident, as the lead instrumentalist in a group is usually the creative force behind the writing and arranging of the songs. A band must be a democracy, with each member able to contribute his or her ideas, but there must be *leadership* as well. There must be one that the others look to for the final word on musical and other decisions. How many times have we talked of famous groups, and heard it said that it was "really his band." Just remember that the democratic way of deciding things is the best way in a band situation, even if one person may be the leader. In some cases, you may have the good fortune to have a band so versatile that several members are able to take turns singing lead and sharing the spotlight. This can make for very interesting performances, but it's important that you not lose sight of the band's overall direction. One band member's music may stray too far from the original concept you all had, and needless to say, this is a situation to be dealt with *very* diplomatically if you don't want to hurt any feelings!

Above all, it's important to keep your rehearsals an even balance of fun and work. Combine time to work on actual songs with time for just jamming and being openly creative with each other. This playful time of jamming and experimenting will prove to be a rich source of inspiration for new ideas, and in the long run will most likely be the most valuable time you spend together.

PERFORMING

Inevitably, there will come a time when you will feel that performing your music in public is the right step to take. At the entry–level of clubs to play, you will usually be required to play mostly "cover" material. That is, you'll play popular and current heavy metal tunes that everyone (especially the management) can relate to. I was frequently faced with this problem in my early performing days when I had a lot of original material I wanted to perform, but I had to play a lot of popular tunes that I didn't even enjoy. As long as you keep the percentage high in favor of the cover tunes, however, you'll always be able to throw in a few of your originals when it feels right. In the long run, the crowd will start to become as familiar with your own songs as they are with the jukebox hits, and don't be surprised if you start to hear some requests being yelled!

Most likely, your band's initial public appearance will be opening the show for a band that already has a following, and whose audience will be there to see *them*, not you. This has its positive aspects as well as negative ones. Indeed, the opening band gets to play a shorter time than the "headliner," but what a great chance to impress their crowd and "blow them away!" Also, by opening for a popular group, you're at least guaranteed an audience—something that may take you a while to develop on your own. While there definitely is a certain degree of pressure on you as an opening act, think of the pressure on the headliners. They are the ones everyone is *expecting* to be good, while you have the chance to pleasantly surprise them! Best of all, if you impress the club owner, or the person who books the place, you'll most likely get asked to come back, possibly as the headliner next time!

Forming and Working With a Band

This happened to me in Woodstock, New York when I was sixteen years old. The year was 1969, and there was a hot music scene in this little upstate town that I wanted to join. I was just starting college in Philadelphia, and my band, "Steel," was living with me. We decided to go to Woodstock and take a look around, hear some music, and possibly make some contacts. Since we had no engagements booked, we didn't even bring so much as a drumstick with us. We wandered into a club called the Sled Hill Cafe, which was a hot spot in town for good music. A great group called "Bang," headed by guitar-wiz Buzzy Feiten, was playing an electrified set, and this served to inspire us more. When their break between sets came, I got up the nerve (which I had plenty of!) to go up and ask them if we could use *their* equipment and play two or three of our tunes during the break. They went along with it and although we felt uncomfortable playing on alien equipment and were understandably a little nervous, we got quite a good response from the crowd and the club owner himself! We went back to Philadelphia that night feeling triumphant believing that we had cracked the shell necessary to get into the Woodstock scene, and that we'd soon be working there on a regular basis.

Unfortunately, months went by with no sign of the follow-up phone calls we expected from the club, so we eventually made another trip back there. When we walked in and the club owner found out who we were, he went crazy! He said that he'd been *dying* to book us in the club for weeks, but lost our phone number, and wasn't even quite sure of our group name. To make a long story short, we became regulars there, actually commuting back and forth between Philly and Woodstock, and I began to make a name for myself there with my guitar prowess. Keep in mind that in Woodstock at that time, the audience could consist of a number of musical luminaries, from Paul Butterfield to The Band, any of whom could change my life in music forever, so this was very crucial for me. As it turned out, it proved to be a pivotal point for me, and I even ended up moving to Woodstock the following year to pursue my career as a guitarist, backing up many of the well-known acts who were based there at the time.

I should also point out that Woodstock was a much freer community, where clubs encouraged the original material many artists in town wrote and performed, and a cover band was almost never to be found. If there is a place near you with a scene such as this, where freedom of expression is encouraged more than in your average club scene, by all means try to play there as much as possible. However, a word to the wise: clubowners can become a really annoying part of your life if you let them. They can be arrogant, cheap, and almost any other bad quality you can imagine when it comes to dealing with musicians. Others can be very kind and respectful. Unfortunately, the latter is quite hard to come by, as I can attest from my years of performing! Still, when all is said and done, if you're bringing in the clientele, you have a much better chance at calling the shots and getting what you want, whether it's more money, better accommodations, or what have you.

Experience in front of audiences will best dictate what kind of show to put on. The reactions you get are the best barometers for judging much of your material and your performance of it. It's also a good idea to make tapes of your gigs for you to listen to and evaluate after the show. This is a good morale booster (something *all* bands need) because it keeps your communication open and frank, and enables you to gloat over or laugh about what you played! Of course, if you want to get a little fancier, you can actually videotape your performances. This will help you critique the visual aspects of your show as well as the musical.

Your Continued Growth

We've covered a lot of ground over the course of this book, which is why I find it hard to believe someone can fully grasp the material after the first reading. For this reason, I encourage you to keep going over the material until it makes sense to you. Everyone must learn at his or her own pace, and you certainly must not feel compelled to learn the material in precisely the order that I have presented it. You may find, for example, that some of the advanced material may come more easily to you than say, a simple blues lick; or that lead guitar in general may be your forte as opposed to rhythm. This is healthy since most musicians end up specializing in one aspect of an instrument and the earlier this uniqueness exposes itself, the better. However, you should be able to get a hold on most of the material in this book since it was carefully put together to be the best heavy metal package possible for you. What you choose to do with it is entirely up to you.

I feel especially strong about understanding the roots of heavy metal, as opposed to thinking of Van Halen as the beginning of all western music! The early blues and rock and roll forms are the basis behind all that we hear today, and it's important to try to understand this history for *your* playing! I know that my love of these musical forms helped fuel my developing years as a guitarist. Indeed, it is a rare star who hasn't been a musicologist of sorts, seeking out and learning about his or her past guitar heroes. An art form such as music is truly an ever-growing language that depends completely upon what has gone before. Not until we understand where music has come from, can we begin to take it further.

It is also important to remember that heavy metal, though a broad and popular field now, may in time become less popular. For this reason, among others, it's crucial that you do not get too locked into this one form of guitar playing. For example, if you're only playing at very loud volumes, take some time to practice at a very quiet level too. This will help fine-tune your technique quite a bit, and will hopefully help you develop an appetite for playing softly. You can also practice on an acoustic guitar. This helps build up strengths, as it takes more physical energy to project clean notes from an acoustic guitar than an electric guitar. I find that when I take an acoustic guitar with me on a trip, I return to find that an electric becomes almost *too* easy for me to play! My fingers become a bit muscle-bound and more acquainted with the harder playing required on the acoustic guitar.

Most of all, I hope this book has helped stir your imagination as far as your guitar playing and career are concerned. I can tell you from years of experience that "it ain't easy out there," and the more incentive you have to succeed, the better off you'll be. Above all, play for yourself, let the music come from the heart, and be happy. If we can't achieve these kinds of goals, what's the point? Good luck to you!

Discography

To enhance the process of learning heavy metal guitar, I have provided a list of "essential listening" in various categories that will help give you a "balanced diet." In order to keep in mind the roots of heavy metal, you should be sure to listen to lots of blues and early rock guitar to help give you a more well-rounded perspective on the instrument, and where it has been before you. Happy listening!

BLUES

Mike Bloomfield

Blonde on Blonde (with Bob Dylan) CBS 00841)
Bringing It All Back Home (with Bob Dylan) (CBS 09128)
East-West (with the Paul Butterfield Blues Band) (Elektra 7315-2)
Highway 61 Revisited (with Bob Dylan) (CBS 09189)
The Paul Butterfield Blues Band (Elektra 7294-2)
Super Session (with Al Kooper and Steve Stills) (CBS 09701)

Buddy Guy

Drinkin' TNT 'N' Smokin' Dynamite! (with Junior Wells) (Blind Pig 1182)
A Man and the Blues (Vanguard 79272)

Robert Johnson

King of the Delta Blues Singers (CBS 62456) (CBS 30034)

B.B. King

The Best of B.B. King (MCA 27074)
Completely Well (MCA 27009)
Live and Well (MCA 27008)
Live at the Regal (MCA 27006)

Otis Rush

Cold Day in Hell (Delmark 638)
Right Place, Wrong Time (Hightone 8007)

EARLY ROCK AND HEAVY METAL GUITAR

Chuck Berry

Chuck Berry's Golden Decade (Chess 1514)

Jeff Beck

Beck-ola (Epic 26478)
Beck's Guitar Shop (Epic 44313)
Blow by Blow (Epic 33409)
There and Back (Epic 35684)
Truth (Epic 26413)

Eric Clapton

Bluesbreakers (with John Mayall) (London 50009)
Disraeli Gears (with Cream) (RSO 3010)
461 Ocean Boulevard (RSO 4801)
Fresh Cream (with Cream) (RSO 3009)
Layla (with Derek and the Dominos) (RSO 3801)
Slowhand (RSO 3030)
Wheels of Fire (with Cream) (RSO 3802)

Bo Diddley

Go Bo Diddley (Checker 9196)
Have Guitar, Will Travel (Checker 9187)

Jimi Hendrix

Are You Experienced? (Reprise 6261)
Axis: Bold as Love (Reprise 6281)
Band of Gypsys (Capitol 472)
Electric Ladyland (Reprise 6307)

Jimmy Page (of Led Zeppelin)

CODA (Swan Song 90051)
Houses of the Holy (Atlantic 19130)
In Through the Out Door (Swan Song 16002)
Led Zeppelin (Atlantic 19126)
Led Zeppelin II (Atlantic 19127)
Led Zeppelin III (Atlantic 19128)
Led Zeppelin IV (Atlantic 19129)
Physical Graffiti (Swan Song 200)
Presence (Swan Song 8416)
The Song Remains the Same (Swan Song 201)

Leslie West (of Mountain)

Avalanche (Columbia 33088)
Best of Mountain (Columbia 32079)
Twin Peaks (Columbia 32818)

CONTEMPORARY HEAVY METAL

Vivian Campbell

Slide It In (with Whitesnake) (Geffen 4018)
Whitesnake (Geffen 24099)

Warren DiMartini (of Ratt)

Dancin' Undercover (Atlantic 81683-1)
Out of the Cellar (Atlantic 80143-1)
RATT (Atlantic 90245-1)

Bruce Kulick (of Kiss)

Animalize (Mercury 822495)
Crazy Nights (Mercury 832626)
Hot in the Shade (Mercury 838913)

George Lynch (of Dokken)

Back for the Attack (Elektra 60735)
Beast from the East (Elektra 60823)

Discography

Breaking the Chains (Elektra 60290)
Tooth and Nail (Elektra 60376)
Under Lock and Key (Elektra 60458)

Yngwie Malmsteen & Rising Force

Marching Out (Polydor 825733)
Odyssey (with Joe Lynn Turner) (Polydor 835451)
Rising Force (Polydor 825324)
Trilogy (Polydor 831073)

Vinnie Moore

Mind's Eye (Schrapnel 1027)
Time Odyssey (Squawk/Polygram 834634)

Joe Satriani

Flying in a Blue Dream (Relativity 1015)
Surfing with the Alien (Relativity 8193)

Steve Vai

Eat 'Em and Smile (with David Lee Roth) (Warner Bros. 25470)
Passion and Warfare (Relativity 1037)
Skyscraper (with David Lee Roth) (Warner Bros. 25671)
Slip of the Tongue (with Whitesnake) (Geffen 24249)

Eddie Van Halen

Diver Down (Warner Bros. 3677)
Fair Warning (Warner Bros. 3540)
5150 (Warner Bros. 25394)
1984 (Warner Bros. 23985)
OU812 (Warner Bros. 25732)
Van Halen (Warner Bros. 3075)
Van Halen II (Warner Bros. 3312)
Women and Children First (Warner Bros. 3415)